MINIATURE SYMPHONIES

FJ GOULDNER

YOU'RE A FANTASTIC
POET! KEEP
SLAMMING.

PEACE!

MINIATURE SYMPHONIES

This book is for music lovers everywhere.

Turn that shit up!

This book is also for estranged family members everywhere.

Wake the fuck up!

INTRO:

This book was written under the influence of music. These songs are all symphonic in their own way within their own genres. I listened to these works repeatedly during the writing of this book and was thoroughly inspired by each.

Music is a huge part of what I do. I hear a distinct melody in my head whenever I write something. This however is the first attempt at simultaneous discovery while listening to specific music.

Each song inspired the corresponding story below.

None of these tracks or their corresponding stories are phony or small in any way. In fact, this book is not for the small, petty or phony. If you fall into any of those 3 categories run along now.

You've been duly warned.

I hope you enjoy Kind Readers.

Section One:

Musical Inspiration

Symphony No.1 in C Major, Op. 21: III. Menuetto-Allegro Molto e Vivace-Beethoven/Tbilisi Symphony Orchestra

A BRUTAL SNAPSHOT

A man begins to slowly lose his mind. He is told he is wrong about everything. His perception of affairs is horribly off. No one agrees with what he is going through.

Then he wakes from his several decades slumber and notices that he is indeed completely right. The people around him have been wasting his time and sapping his energy, telling him it is not them, it is him.

Rick Van Winkle spent 30 plus years under the assumption that to feel, care, help, and have compassion for others all the time was weak, or at best a bit misguided and idealistic. Then when he woke from his long sleep he realized it most definitely was not him. It was the company he kept. None of them felt as deeply or realized the supreme importance of being a help to your fellow man.

His family were the worst offenders. He had always been there for all of them but when it came time to ask them for help they vanished and left a note:

"Fend for yourself Master Rick. We only want to associate with you when you are flush and do not have need of our help. We are unwilling. We must take care of our own."

Master Rick wept for an instant then in his mind's eye he lopped away all false friends and family impostors like they were dead branches on his precious tree of life and he began again.

*This story was inspired by the realization that unfortunately most people (including family) do not make time for those they love. Some friends and family make no effort whatsoever and the person who does make the effort comes to the startling realization that they are alone and the relationship in question is in no way reciprocal. Never has been.

This is a story of disappointment and pain. But also of liberation. Symphonic in its intensity.

Symphony No. 1 in C major, Op. 21: IV Finale: Adagio-Allegro Molto e Vivace-Beethoven/Tbilisi Symphony Orchestra

WELCOME TO DADVILLE

Susanna Harper set foot in Dadville for the first time in December and she thought it to be the saddest place on the face of the earth. But somehow an unmistakeable joy existed simultaneously. The town was founded and solely populated by divorced men and their children were visiting for Christmas or so it seemed.

The total lack of an adult female presence was rather strange and of course the rules of the community were also rather bizarre. If you fell for someone or became involved in another relationship you were asked to depart and were fully expected to leave town within no more than a week.

As a trained reporter Susanna knew that nothing was ever really black and white. There were always several shades of gray, and her's began to manifest when she met Orville Meacham. She quickly forgot her primary assignment to write about this rather unique community for the Sentinel, her newspaper. When Orville took her from behind on the back porch by the smoldering woodstove she even forgot she was a writer for a time.

Nights of unbridled passion followed. Raw lovemaking like she had never experienced. She thought it would go on forever.

Until one warm, sunny afternoon in spring when Orville took her out for a romantic picnic in the deep forest. Very shortly after they both climaxed Orville bounded to his feet and pulled up his trousers in one fluid motion, while looking down at her adoringly. She was still completely helpless lying naked on their picnic blanket when she noticed the townsmen encircling her and approaching slowly from every direction.

*This story was inspired by my wife. We often found ourselves driving through a small upstate New York town by the name of Dadville. My wife saw this as a sad little village possibly populated by divorced or widowed men visiting with their children together at a fast food restaurant on a Sunday with no adult women present.

I of course skewed this pure melancholic idea and made it horrifically symphonic.

Sermon-Drowning Pool

SOAPBOX

A lone man with a powerful voice stands on his soapbox shouting in the center of the town square. He is so charismatic people actually begin to listen. What he is saying makes sense.

The crowd grows larger throughout the afternoon. Soon throngs of people surround the man. He seems to gain momentum as more people stop to listen.

"I plant seeds, but it is up to you to water them!" was the last thing he said. Then he simply disappeared into the crowd and was gone.

Not a single spectator watered anything. They were only happy being spoon fed raw information. The man's message was powerful but not powerful enough to wake the people from their deep, somnambulistic habit energy. Words in the end were just words.

*This song reminds me of a crowd being thoroughly inspired and dreaming of all the changes they will make after hearing a powerful speaker. Then returning home and changing nothing. Back to their usual routine of lethargy and early death. Disgusted with themselves but unwilling or unable to move a muscle.

Preaching the End of the World-Chris Cornell

SOLO

The end is near, yet he is still alone.

He can't believe it. The end of the fucking world and here he sits. Jesus Christ what a downer!

It started out as a very promising life. He was surrounded by family that loved him. He grew, was married, and had several children of his own. But it was all a facade. Some sort of cruel joke. One by one they all abandoned him. He had always been there for every one of them. Loyal to a fault. They were not loyal. They were not even kind. Perhaps even here at the very end he was better off without them.

Yet he longed for some sort of companionship. What or who did he need? All he knew is that he was tired of his own company. It was time to converse. To hear someone else's voice and opinions for a change. To hear a whole new set of ideas. God! Why did he wait so long? It took the imminent destruction of the entire world to make him realize that he needed a friend?

At least a single friend.

Unfortunately he waited too long. During the preparation and choosing process he was so particular that the Earth imploded on itself before he could make up his mind.

*This song is just plain melancholy. It makes me sad every time I give it a listen. Imagine someone so alone that they would need to seek out a friend to share the end of the world with.

Tragic.

So What-Miles Davis

TECHNIQUE

Everything he does is loaded with technique but he has transcended technique through constant practice. Now he has become something else. Something almost perfect. Graceful beyond description really.

Daily he works at it. Daily he gets better. More proficient, further along the path. He has become an improvisational instrument. All flowing movement and rich artistry. A skillful master craftsman.

As he slides his shovel into the earth once again he keeps one thing foremost in his mind:

Someone will lie forever in this hole I am digging.

*For me Miles represents perfection and passion in art. He knew his trumpet and what he wanted to come out of it. He was a consummate craftsman. Pushing sonic boundaries and composing stunning frameworks from which to launch into beautifully passionate improvisations.

So What perfectly puts forth the idea that you must practice for countless hours before you can improvise.

There is no life without discipline.

Katharine Hepburn

Back In Black-AC/DC

THE BEGINNING AND THE END

Stealing booze, cigarettes, and later drugs from a few choice relatives and aquaintances. Attending parties and enecting the lame 80's pop shit. "Fuck Kajagoogoo motherfucker! The crew is here now!"

Burning irreverence and a total lack of respect for the establishment. The idea of tuning in, turning on, and dropping out morphing into the desire to utterly destroy. Appetite for Destruction my ass. More like Appetite for Annihilation.

Drinking and drugging with total abandon until realizing that you had been duped. The establishment wanted you drunk, helpless, and out of control. That's how you became less of a threat.

No more. You are far more dangerous sober. You're back and better than ever! The fuckers tried but they couldn't take you out. You're like a fucking cockroach after a nuclear war. Ahh... breathe in that beautiful green shit.

Improvise, adapt, overcome!

*Back In Black was the second album I ever owned. The first was Bruce Springsteen's The River. Both on vinyl but they elicited two totally different responses from my parents. My parents were ok with The Boss but they were not ok with AC/DC at all. However, upon first listen I knew that things would never be the same again. From the first chime of Hell's Bells and my father screaming to turn that garbage down to side 2 with Back and Black blaring its rhythmic defiance I, (right there and then) became a juvenile delinquent.

Genesis w/Phil Collins-Turn It On Again

WALKING THE STREETS

When I was a wayward delinquent teenager a few friends seemed to always broaden my horizons beyond the constant quest for alcohol, drugs, and easy ass. Sull was one of these folks.

From Genesis and Roxy Music, to Miles Davis and John Coltrane as we left our teen years. Sull was always growing and searching musically and any encounter with him was a learning experience.

When we were younger Sull witnessed the onset of the first hip-hop generation and he became inspired by these rebels. He took to walking the streets with his boom box. But he wasn't playing Kool Moe Dee or Run DMC. No, he was blasting such tunes as War Pigs from Black Sabbath or The Ripper from Judas Priest. And of course Turn It On Again from Genesis. Some of the looks he got were priceless. But Sull didn't care. He was tuned into the music. The music that went everywhere with him.

*The last I heard Sull was a family man and although he should have somehow been in the music business, necessity dictated otherwise and he had to provide for his family. I seriously doubt that any other mailman alive has such an encyclopedic knowledge of music. It warms my heart to imagine Sull on his dedicated mail route still listening to music, still walking the streets, although I doubt he stilll carries a boombox. But maybe, just maybe.

Wake Up- Rage Against the Machine

THE REVOLUTION BEGINS

It's been going on since the very beginning. There is a cycle. The people rebel against the powers that be, the rebels become the powers that be, they become corrupt and complacent, the people rebel once again. Nothing new has been attempted. Nothing at all ever really changes.

When a new group takes power they plug themselves into the old outdated structures built by their endless line of predecessors and of course become just as oppressive and corrupt.

People are not meant to be ruled. Hierarchy and nationalism are viruses created by the rich and privileged to keep the lower classes under some semblance of control. And boy have they spread like wildfire! Those two insane ideas have infiltrated every aspect of human existence. From religion to the workplace. From the martial arts dojo, to the family hearth. There seems to always be a master to answer to. Don't let me get started on the legal system. Judges, police officers, and other officials are a thoroughly laughable bunch. Demanding respect for a profession they chose to enter? Strange. The same goes for the military. Last time I checked there was no longer a draft in effect. They are volunteers that believed the vultures (recruiters) lies.

I've said it once. I'll say it a million times; NATIONALISM IS A DISEASE. And it has killed billions. It's time for a horizontal structure. No masters, no hierarchy, or the insanity of Nationalism. Just regular people. Partners really. All helping one another and healing from this nightmare that has been mislabeled: CIVILIZATION.

*This song reminds me of rebellion. And accidents of birth. How could we be proud of where we were born? It wasn' t like we chose it. How could anyone be willing to die for that totally abstract concept? Because we were told we should be willing that's how. And we bought that shit hook, line, and sinker.

Held Down-De La Soul

THE ONE

Intense momentum in the streets of the city. Movement everywhere. Cabs and cars, and bikes and buses. Boxtrucks and construction vehicles, and people. Of course people are slamming to and fro passing each other, barely noticing that their paths have crossed, living their lives in close proximity to one another and barely caring or knowing much of anything or anyone at all.

The sense of community has gone by the wayside. It is truly every man and woman for themselves. But there are always exceptions. Good folks concerned with their environment and those who are in it. That is why humanity always prevails. The one. The single individual that follows their heart rather than the hive mind.

Praise be to the outlaws and iconoclasts that move us forward. Why must we first vilify them before their genius is recognized? Why must they be called criminals before their status as savior is cemented? Why is this always the way? I suppose our own history has taught us nothing.

*This song reminds me of a loner that transcends the bullshit of his experiences and upbringing to create a life for himself. He refuses to use excuses.

Lancaster Gate-Enter the Haggis

YES TO LIFE

Saying yes to life is the only important response to what you face every day. Life has a way of smacking you upside the head over and over again. But if you find yourself standing at the end of the day, still alive and breathing, you must say yes or you are wasting precious time.

No bitching, stop complaining stop being petty and own your existence. Someone always has it worse. Do I understand why beautiful, innocent little children get diseases and die, while waste of space mean, vindictive people that are basically a walking bag of addictions go on poisoning the world with their constant negativity? No. I don't. But I can tell you that I refuse to waste what little time I have on this earth bitching, complaining, and unnecessarily mourning people and things that are no longer alive or part of my life.

I will say Yes! I will let go of negative unhealthy things and celebrate life for those who are no longer here. I am full of joy for whatever comes next. And if I cash out anytime soon mourn if you will but never ever use my passing as an excuse for not moving on. If you mourn someone for a lifetime then it is two lives that have been wasted. I will always be present in joy.

*My wife and I saw Enter the Haggis in Utica, N.Y. purchased the album and cranked Lancaster Gate out of our minivan through the city streets all night. Such a positive, hopeful song! Taking the bagpipes away from death and giving them back to life.

Without a single word.

Raised By Horses-Clutch

WRECK YOUR FACE

Entering the room he dancex around wildly and slapped the first suit across the face hard.

Whirling rapidly he kicked the second suit square in the jaw making it snap loudly.

He approached the third dude and shouted a screech so shrill even I covered my ears.

My brother would be damned if these music industry types lured me away to record off the farm.

God I love this crazy fuck. Naa, he's right. I ain't going anywhere. Our music wouldn't be ours if we sold out.

We both chased the third guy across the pasture and all three of 'em got in the black Escalade and boogied.

"You can't get our dirt, muddy, farm rock anywhere but here you fuckers!" my brother shouted, laughing.

"Yee fucking ha!"

*This song just reminds me of a free for all orchestrated by a man who is free and sick of people trying to take his freedom away to bottle it up for the masses.

Hotel California-Eagles

TRAPPED

Entering, she noticed how old and dilapidated the place was. Things were worn and crumbling wherever her gaze fell. But somehow she knew that this is where she belonged.

Years passed and people came and they went, she remained. Like a fixture. Put 2 more legs on her and she'd be a piece of furniture soon.

Before she had been an inveterate wanderer. She moved every 6 months or so. But when she arrived here she stopped abruptly. A feeling of warmth enveloped her. A sad resignation. Soft defeat. This, as they say, was it. And she just knew.

Movement was over. Travelling all done. Now it was time to sit and write about her adventures. She would live her life exclusively in the past from now on. Sadness wrapped its defeated arms tightly around her and afterwards she began to write.

*This song has always made me think of being trapped after a lifetime of travel. A sad, defeated song that bargoers have been singing at the top of their lungs for decades. Every time it comes on the radio or jukebox I cringe. But it never gets changed. We are trapped by its melancholy songcraft.

Resistance is futile.

Save Your Scissors-City and Colour

UNREQUITED

A lost love is a destructive thing. It taints a life like nothing else. Things are measured by it. Decisions made because of it.

Many happy memories. Beauty, passion, love. Being somewhere in an entirely different way. Noticing how life is entirely brilliant. Marveling that you love and are loved.

Then it is over. No real explanation. The thing has just run its course. You stand, stunned. Heart ripped directly out of your chest. There are no words. Just feelings. They all hit you like a rogue wave and flip you upside down like a shell on the beach.

Then just a disembodied voice saying goodbye on an answering machine in a sunny afternoon livingroom.

*This song reminds me of a lost love. A thing of beauty reduced to the reality of selfishness and the unbridled desire to escape.

The Mob Rules-Black Sabbath w/Dio

A CALL TO ARMS

A rage filled, immediate up-tempo blast of metal sounded through the loudspeakers. It was as though the guitar solo was instructing the crowd assembled to riot.

The people had had enough of the lies and constant deception. It was time for them to take their country back. By force if necessary.

There would be no more voting, no more partisanship, no ridiculous media bias or spin doctoring. These people would be removed.

Rebellion hung heavy in the air and the so-called elected officials trembled in fear. They knew their time was short.

For the first time since the birth of the American Nation not a single soul voted in any election. No one ruled. No one represented. Every free man and woman was responsible for themselves and their families. No one else. And the country fluorished. A government for the people, by the people.

At long last.

*This strong revolutionary piece of metal has always represented a structural sea change of some sort or another. I imagine it being blasted through a truck's loudspeakers as the truck pierces the fence in front of 1600 Pennsylvania Avenue headed directly up the lawn to the great White House.

This song was also part of Demonaut's repertoire. The powerful but short lived heavy metal band I sang with in the '80's. This story is for Dom, Mike, Donny, and Tommy my bandmates. It was a blast boys. Horns up!!!

Back In The Saddle-Aerosmith

AXIS

A man sitting alone in a room quiet except for the slow sharpening of an axe blade and the scraping sound of metal on metal. The room is illuminated by a single bare bulb protruding from a lamp with no shade.

The man sharpens the axe slowly, methodically, he is in no hurry.

Off somewhere in the distance he hears the unmistakeable sound of the streets. A siren, a gunshot, a horn blaring, a woman's scream.

His right hand comes up to touch the tip of the sharpened blade. A single drop of blood leaks from his fingertip. He smiles widely and screams:

"I'm Back!!!"

*I often imagined this song as the soundtrack for a short film. The beginning of this song is very ominous and would fit the scene perfectly. Listen to it and read this piece and you will see.

Back Door Man-The Doors

BETRAYED

As a friend, husband, lover, brother, family member, I require 3 things: Caring, Kindness, and Loyalty. If you can't provide these then I don't want to know you.

Somehow, for the majority of my life I have been surrounded by fools. Both friends and family members have used, abused, and taken me for granted. This will not happen again. I will guard my sanity, privacy, and kindness from here on in with a fierce vengeance. No one will betray me again. It will not be possible.

Here's to starting over. No negativity, no one-sided relationships, no more betrayal allowed. Come forward those of you who are truly genuine and have a true friend 'til the end.

*This song has always reminded me of someone being proud of being a vicious, backstabbing bastard. May all of those folks that create drama where none exists and go through their lives selfishly treating others according to their moods and whims quietly slide into a corner and disappear.

The Ambrose Law-Ancestors

BLACK, WHITE, AND GRAINY

The photo shows 3 smiling youths on a beach in winter. 2 males 1 female. They appear very happy. The female wears a knit poncho her black hair flowing in the wind. The men are both in denim jackets, one facing the woman smiling, the other facing the camera smiling and winking.

The woman would die from an extremely debilitating case of MS in a wheelchair, blind and incontinent at the age of 35. The man looking at the woman smiling committed a particularly brutal armed robbery of a convenience store killing 3 customers and a sales clerk. He will spend life in prison. The man smiling directly into the camera and winking overdosed on heroin and was found cold and dead in his run down apartment on 60th street.

The 60's were a promise. The 70's a lie, and the 80's were a reckoning. All 3 people in the photo were somehow assigned a decade. All died young with one thing in common. The happiness they shared that winter day at the beach.

*Photographs are capable of capturing moments in a life, but not life itself. This song reminds me of tragedy. And a person looking at a photograph recalling happier times, but feeling sorrow because on the particular day the photo was taken these 3 people had their chance to go in a different direction.

After he took their picture that day he did.

Once In a Lifetime-Talking Heads

DEATH DANCE

He is not at all clear on what happened. He was vaguely aware of anger, depression, a loose grasp on reality. Things ceasing to mean anything or make sense.

He was dancing, stomping his feet, and shaking his ass. The music washed over him but it didn't clean his body like water would have. There was blood everywhere. He was covered in it.

The clock struck 12 and he continued dancing in a large puddle of blood. He asked himself a question out loud: "If I can't remember it, did it happen?"

He started laughing hysterically. Louder and longer he laughed until he was shuddering like a lunatic. He kept dancing. He puked, pissed himself, had a bowel movement in his pants and fell to the floor. He pretended to swim in the blood, vomit, piss, and feces.

It all came back to him in a rush. He had snapped. Killed his entire family and a few others on his block who had wondered about the commotion they heard. Everybody was buried neatly in a row in his backyard.

He heard sirens off in the distance and he danced. He was back on his feet and he could not stop dancing.

*This song always reminds me of a progressive descent into insanity.

Tush-ZZ Top

DRAG

Betty Blue felt real good. She took the curves and straightaways like the smooth body of a woman.

His foot pressed hard on her accelerator and sped her whole body up considerably.

The steering wheel glided effortlessly through his hands and he felt the rich smoothness of its wood.

But what got him going, what excited him most was her gearshifter. Long, slender, strong, it felt powerful in his hand and was the true key to Betty Blue in all her sweetness and power. When he grabbed it she shuddered all over. That's really where he felt her response to his attentions.

They drove together to the spot. Other vehicles and drivers were there waiting.

Betty Blue roared past all of the competition with ease. It wasn't even a contest. She did drag better than anyone he had ever known. Better than any car he had ever owned.

She was fucking beaautiful.

*This song is truly one of my favorites. I sang it many times with a few classic rock outfits over the years. The only complaint I have ever had about it is its length. It's too fucking short! It's like a drag race instead of a course. It's so tight and hard driving we all want just one more verse.

The Chain-Fleetwood Mac

DRIFTERMAN

Slowly he trudges into a western town. He is on foot with a small shoulder pack slung low. Dust blows around him as he walks.

A handful of the town's baleful residents witness his arrival. No one thinks anything of it.

He makes his way to the nearest saloon and orders a soda. Whiskey makes a man reckless and stupid.

Later in the evening he makes his presence known. He finds her beneath large, sweaty, pig of a man. He inserts the railroad spike into the base of Piggy's skull with one swift hammer blow.

His daughter did not make this choice. His degenerate gambling made the choice for her. Poker had turned his little girl into a harlot. He was determined to atone for his mistake. Woe to those who would interfere with his process.

*In the past, while listening to this song I always imagined a lone drifter entering an old western town during the approaching dusk. His mission evolved over repeated listenings.

The Lamb Lies Down on Broadway-Genesis w/Peter Gabriel

FED UP AND FINALLY FREE

A middle aged man walks the New York City streets and becomes hyper aware of the rushing masses, the cacaphony, the uselessness of all of it.

He suddenly realizes with a start that the first half of his life was all about this madness and he wants no more of it.

An old song he remembers mystically calls him to Broadway. He hears the piano echoing in his head as he breaks into a run the final few blocks.

When he reaches the famous Boulevard he stops in his tracks on the sidewalk thinking of his past life.

Abruptly he steps off the sidewalk into the center of the street and lies down stretching out his arms wide as if about to be crucified. He smiles as he realizes that he will never be a part of regular society again.

*This story symbolizes hope and the release I have always felt when I have heard Peter Gabriel belt out the line that gives the track its title. Ask yourself these questions Kind Readers;

What would life be like if hope and the desire to create became your currency?

What would you make of your life if you stopped in your tracks RIGHT NOW and changed direction?

Serenity-Godsmack

FIRST DAYS CLEAN

The color has been drained out of everything. Meaning is gone. There is no point to waking up and drawing breath. Ceaseless nothingness. A new life they say. More like death. No desire to be this hyper aware. Before I noticed little or nothing. Just how I like it. Oblivious. Yes, I long to revisit oblivion.

Time passes slowly. The seconds crawl. Why would anyone want to do this? This state of being is fucking miserable. No wonder why people continue to get fucked up.

It's better.

A good day arrives unexpectedly. A feeling of pure harmony washes over everything and everyone. Life is miraculous. All is connected. Now I understand. Now I see why people seek sobriety. I am proud to have achieved it. What will my life be now? So much potential. Limitless possibilities. Thankful for this great gift.

Tomorrow brings more pain and uncertainty. Using seems to be a good idea. The perfect method to alleviate the lack of motivation and depression. Up, down, grateful, disgusted, all pieces of the early sobriety puzzle.

Hang tough.

*This song has a sort of ominous feel but the mere word Serenity is enough to remind a long time recovering addict/alcoholic that those first tentative days will pay huge dividends if you devote yourself to recovery.

North Country Blues-Bob Dylan

GHOST TOWN

The factory kept this town afloat. Everything and everyone was humming all the time. Life moved along, there was no time for dissatisfaction or complaining. There was work to be done, fun to be had, families to care for and bills to be paid.

Then one day the factory was slated for shutdown. Sure we protested, and picketed, and marched on the owner's homes. But they closed it anyway, with no regard for what it would cause.

Folks left. Just up and disappeared it seemed. The entire town froze dead in its tracks. You could feel the pain and sorrow with the lack of every step.

Many small American towns fold in on themselves like this. They put all their eggs in one basket and the good times are quickly replaced by bad when the lifeblood gets drained out.

Booze takes on a more important role and many will go to an an early grave because there's nowhere to be and their drinking increases wildly.

And while this town breathes its last and burns; the bankers, owners, and various fatcats light their cigars off of the burning embers.

*Dylan captured the travails of a mining town perfectly. He was 22 and clearly a conduit or "hollow bone" for the Creator, because he had almost no real life experience when he wrote this.

It is 1963.

It is haunting.

Let It Go-Def Leppard

GET IN

A young long-haired man lets his beautiful girl into his 60's era Firebird and gently closes the door behind her.

He climbs into the driver's seat with a huge smile on his face.

Soon they are on the NYS Thruway and the speedometer is steadily climbing. 70... 80... 90... 100... Everything around them becomes a blur. They hold hands. No words are necessary.

... 120 ... 140 ... 180 faster and faster. The sight of the Tappan Zee Bridge up ahead.

Directly through the guardrail pierces the flying Firebird and down into the Hudson below. There is no tragedy. No sorrow. They planned this. Together. They simply did not want to hang around. They saw what their lives were bound to become and they wanted none of it. The best times they would ever have were already in the past.

They survived the impact and courage briefly turned to fear as they began drowning. But they embraced each other as their breath gave out simultaneously.

"Dear?" the old woman asked quizzically.

"Yes?" the old man answered.

"What were you daydreaming about?"

"Oh nothing sweetheart. Nothing at all," he said, as his mint condition Firebird approached the Tappan Zee Bridge.

*This song always reminded me of a mutual suicide pact. And it was the last Leppard album with balls and bite before Mutt Lange destroyed the band. Did they make a commercial suicide pact?

Bohemian Rhapsody-Queen

GENRE JUMP

What's to say you have to fit somewhere? That you need to pigeonhole yourself into a preconceived hole. The more I experience life as I grow older I realize that some people just don't fit. They are natural shapeshifters. More comfortable with change than any idea of belonging or fitting in. It has taken me a lifetime to realize that this is ok.

Folks look at you strange when you can't define yourself. They need to be able to wrap you up nice and tight and place you in a specific box. If you can't provide this kind of comfortable categorization well then, they will gladly classify you. Yes, you will be filed under dangerous. Subversive even. After all anyone who doesn't fit couldn't possibly belong. That idea is just too scary. Like Jiddu Krishnamurti's approach: "Truth is pathless land." The idea of blazing your own trail, hacking your own path, is like bungee jumping straight into the abyss. Far too frightening. No normal person would do such a thing. It is preposterous to imagine that anyone could function without a clear set of rules and regulations. Dogma is to be sought out. Cherished and passed down through the generations. Nevermind if it makes no sense. Forget about free will. Forget about any sort of freedom at all. Freedom is only an illusion anyway. No one can truly be free. Why seek out what doesn't exist? Be safe. Join the human race.

As a person who has refused to conform the idea of joining the sheeple is the true nightmare. And if membership in the human race requires me to become a worker drone or mindless automaton then I prefer to remain out on the fringes happy, independent, and free.

*This song reminds me of individualistic tendencies. The song itself denies facile categorization. The two suburban dopes Wayne and Garth robbed the song of its epic mystery. Mike Myers understands almost nothing. That is why his films are popular. You are not required to think to understand them.

I like to think. But when Beelzebub puts a devil aside for me I can't help but bang my head right along with the rest of them.

The Rage-Judas Priest

ILLUSION OF THE OUTLANDER

I came here to escape the madness of the homeland. I could not take the pain and opression any longer. I needed to taste freedom. This land appears new and unsullied. There are no rules or strictures here. It is my paradise.

Last night my shelter was burned. I do not understand but I must rebuild. My food stores disappeared and I am very hungry. I must find food soon. Replenish or die.

I awoke hanging from a tree limb. I am very frightened. A man comes into view, a red skinned man, he looks up at me. He looks angry. Well I am angry too. I'm frightened, hungry, and I'm hanging in a tree. He's ruined my paradise.

After what seems like a very long time he cuts me down but leaves my hands bound. He drags me through the forest and brings me before an old man in a makeshift village.

I have become a slave. I am beaten and tortured daily. If there is a hell I'm in it. Days pass and I pray for death.

Instead men like me arrive in ships. I escape my captors with revenge in my heart and go to find my brothers.

*This song reminds me of how there are massive repercussions to how human beings treat each other. The outlander comes to a new land believing it is his. A sense of misguided entitlement. The native believes the land is his. More misguided entitlement. The earth cannot be owned. She is ours. All of ours. We must share her. All the rest is wrong.

Lust for Life-Iggy and the Stooges

HUSTLING

Out the door, down the apartment building stairs, bounding down two steps at a time.

Once out on the street there's a spring in his step. How much can he make today? How much of a risk is he willing to take?

Ah baby, big risks.

Real big.

The hours tick by but the only way he notices is the lengthening of his shadow on the sidewalk. This is him, this is what he does, he knows nothing else.

Shit happens all around him. But it doesn't affect him because he is a survivor. Top of the motherfucking food chain.

Deep down he knows there's gotta be another way of life. Free time, leisure, enjoyment. But he also doubts this other life's existence. Because all he really knows is the hustle.

The way he shoots through life makes the worst workaholic appear lazy as shit.

Will he ever slow down?

Give up the game?

Chances are.........

*This song has always reminded me of scenes from a speed hustler's life. Each day shot out of a cannon and the next day more of the same.

Root Down-Beastie Boys

HUSTLE

Nothing stops him. No one gets in his way. If something or someone decides they will try and be an obstacle he removes them by any means necessary. He leaves a wake of death and destruction wherever he goes but it's just business and nothing more.

Not a single thing in his past indicated that he would become what he has. He was a mediocre student, a nondescript kid drinking and smoking himself silly on the weekends and playing video games and watching semi-sexual and semi- violent movies.

He created himself for one reason and one reason only. The opportunity presented itself. Drugs, women, other deals, murder, racketeering, extortion, it was all the same to him. Just business. Nothing personal.

Your wife is found eviscerated in the front of her car, your family is picked off one by one, the house explodes in a giant ball of flames, you wake up in the hospital with your dick missing, there's only one question you should be asking yourself: "What the hell did I do to deserve this?" Because unfortunately it's ALWAYS the same. You definitely did something. That kind of shit doesn't just happen.

The idea of guilt never even enters the picture. He was a businesssman and there were consequences. It was never personal. As a matter of fact, he never even thought of you or you're dilemma.

*This tune reminds me of matter of fact ruthlessness for some reason. Adam MCA Yauch rest in peace or come back as a Tibetan monk.

If you wish.

Like Suicide-Soundgarden

HOPE

When all is seemingly lost. When even holy men are ready to give up the ghost. There is something that carries them through. A sense, a feeling that no matter what the outside appearance life is joyous and worth living. That those who succumb to the darkness and pain are cowards and have missed the point entirely.

Trials hurt him deeply but make him stronger so he welcomes them. Well not exactly welcomes, but he is grateful for them.

He stands strong but battered, intense. He loves those close to him but refuses to lie. This makes life harder but he presses on because he knows it is right to hold the truth dear.

In time all who vilified him will realize he was the only real soul. Fearless, unrelenting, refusing to lay down and join the status quo. There is no quit in him. He continues despite all odds. He does it because that's what he was born to do.

You would think that people would be drawn to him. They are not. They are afraid because he is the pure, undistilled personification of hope. He will not take no for an answer. He is alive to live. He has no time for pettiness. People shrink from the light he exudes because they realize how much they'd have to change to even approach where he is. They DO NOT want to be reminded of their shortcomings.

For a time he was very angry at everything and everyone that didn't understand. Then one day peace enveloped him and he just let go...

*This tune represents pure hope and dynamic peace for me. It transcends the cowardice of suicide and points to the payoff which is just life itself. And the miraculous ability to draw breath.

Blue Train-John Coltrane

HAPPY TO BE ALIVE

A man bounds out of his small apartment, out of the building, onto the city streets. He seemingly notices everything and everyone. He waves at the newspaper delivery truck, he picks up a paper and leaves extra for the newsstand man. He buys coffee and gives half a bagel and the rest of his cup to a bum. Further down the street he compliments a pretty breakfast waitress as he walks by.

His neighborhood hums because he is in it. Completely, fully, he's a part of it and it's a part of him. He could not imagine living anywhere else. He has thought that if he had to move he would die. That both he and his neighborhood were one and the same, indivisible.

He had certainly found the secret to a happy life. Give your whole self to where you are at the moment. Become a part of something. Stop complaining, find that place, and stay there. Travelling was fine. But if there is no home to come back to what's the point?

That's why he's happy to be alive.

He is home.

*Coltrane's work is complicated and extraordinary but comfortable like a good solid apartment with books everywhere.

Sir Duke-Stevie Wonder

MUSIC IS LIFE

A man dances through a succession of scenes. He is visibly happy. Joyful even. Horns blare as his feet glide. War, despair, death, intolerance, all are transformed into their corresponding positives in this man's wake.

There is music playing all around. The man greets many of the music world's luminaries in his travels as well as many peacemakers and other artists known throughout the world and across time.

The message is clear. Music is the universal language and if this planet is to be healed music shall accomplish it. Open your ears and listen. And dance. Don't ever forget to dance.

*I defy anyone who listens to this song to sit still. A hand will drum, a foot will tap, you may not actually get up and dance but you will feel it all over.

Sweet Miracle-Rush

MOVING THROUGH

How could so much tragedy befall a single human being? Better yet, how could one continue after all of the pain, disappointment, and loss? Movement. That's how. A body at rest is a body dead. Movement is the only thing that cures pain brought on by devastating disappointment and tragic loss. If we remain still we commune with death. Motion is life.

No matter what happens to us in life we must keep moving. There is no other alternative. Death, loss, pain, disappointment can all be remedied (if not cured outright) by an extended solo road trip.

*This song was obviously written by a man who suffered and found salvation in the miracle of movement. That man was Neil Peart from Rush.

Good Grief-Foo Fighters

MOVEMENT

The constant desire for newness. The wretched desire for movement. Always on to the next place, the next house, the next life. After a while you get tired.

Cars, things, people rushing by. Never enough time for any true connection to people, places, or things. It becomes a sort of addiction.

Nomads got nothing on me. At least their movement is seasonal and similar every year. The same basic trajectory becomes familiar no matter how far. My movement has no rhyme or reason. It's like being shot out of a cannon with no idea where the ball will fall.

Hopefully this is it. I truly pray that I have found home. It's no wonder that it lies directly between 3 cities. Atlantic, New York, and Philadelphia. Just in case I get bored.

*This song reminds me of all of the frenetic movement over the past 10 years. 10 houses in 10 years! Moving constantly has become this family's pastime. Belonging nowhere. Not understanding the term HOME in a physical way. Just a sweet idea. A sentiment for the sedentary.

Fight for your Mind - Ben Harper

GRANTED

The blue sky or even if the sky is open and pouring. The sounds and smells of nature and man. A child's sweet smile, a look, a kiss or simple touch of a loved one's hand.

Fresh pain. New experiences. Solitude and a lack of tortured screams and compromised silence.

Stepping out into the wide open world free and trusted to do sane things and make normal decisions. Struggle for these simple things not for things that really make no difference.

The mind is a terribly fragile thing. I know, they tell me this every day. But if I had another chance I would guard my sanity and all that comes with it.

Freedom is the most important thing in my life. These walls are grey and closing in. I'm not the man I once was. Not even the boy. I remember my first tour of this place. I didn't realize I'd never leave.

It's medication time. Time to say goodbye for the rest of the day and part of the night. Until I wake cold in my room knowing fully once again that I've lost my mind, and that there are legions of people out there free to move about as they wish with no appreciation or gratitude for anything.

They say that youth is wasted on the young. They should say that sanity is wasted on the sane.

*This story is dedicated to Greg Pilger. Institutionalized since age 17, and fighting for his mind now for 26 long years. I miss him.

Flying High Again-Ozzy Osbourne

MUSIC LIKE CANDY

When a man does not drink or drug music is like candy. An incredibly strong, sweet, all consuming passionate experience.

Notes pierce the eardrums with pleasure that cannot be accurately described. Nothing like the distorted jumble that blasts into the head when drunk or high.

Listening to music drunk or high is a diluted experience best left to pre-adolescent snotnoses who have never experienced life.

Music can only be understood while totally stone cold sober. Otherwise it loses its strength and is drained of its true power. If you must use to make sense of or enjoy music then what you are listening to is just noise.

*Boot Camp, Great Lakes 1985. Company 377 steps off the bus at a department store to shop for Christmas. I knew why I was there. I had heard no music except for cadence during marches for more than 60 days. I beelined it for the record players. Luckily, someone left an album on the turntable. I moved the needle over and Flying High Again blasted out of the speakers crystal clear. The Company Commander found me and put his hand on the volume knob. I must've looked like he was about to murder a family member. He smiled and turned it up. I had spent the previous 60 days hating this man's guts. In that moment I loved him like a brother.

Music, sweet music.

Can't Find My Way Home-Blind Faith

LEFT AND ABANDONED

Invited to a friend's wedding. All is well. Conventionally beautiful even. He somehow feels very lonely amongst all of these people but he manages his anxiety for a good while.

Then it happens. The switch gets flicked. Somewhere around beer #8 and shot #6 he knows that if he keeps going it will probably be disastrous. Yet he keeps drinking. In this situation knowledge does not translate to power.

He makes a monumental fool of himself. People drive right by and leave him stranded alone in the reception hall parking lot. After a time he begins walking and has no idea where he is going. He is very drunk. He notices he has a Tuxedo on. He suddenly remembers that he was in a wedding and all of his so-called friends left him. He rips off the cummerbund, then the shirt with all of its individual cuff-link like buttons, he has no idea where the jacket has gone. Then he rips off his white t-shirt and kicks off his shoes. He is naked from the waist up and it is cold as hell outside.

Soon he finds himself sort of 'coming to' while walking on a major highway. A pair of young cops pick him up and take him to the station. He remains naked from the waist up and in stocking feet. They give him nothing to cover up. They only snicker. He asks to make a phone call and somehow manages to escape. He eludes the ignorant government functionaries altogether. They never find him. Probably didn't try. He finds a red and black checkered shirt on someone's back porch. Ah warmth. Then he locates a pair of workboots and puts them on.

Tuxedo pants, lumberjack shirt, and workboots, what a sight he must've made.

A cabbie agrees to take him the 2 hours it will take to get home. When he arrives 5 blocks from his house he skips out on the fare and the cabbie attempts to chase him. But he knows these streets and he manages to escape again.

Weeks later, the friend who invited him to the wedding laughs heartily at his drunkenness and misfortune. He never hung out with this 'friend' again. He knew then that he really didn't have any friends. Friends don't abandon you. They take care of you no matter what. This former friend never knew the kind of friend he was. That he would take a bullet for him. He never realized.

Until now.

*This song always reminds me of the loneliness of false friendships. And the apathy and sadness that comes when someone realizes that they are the court jester of a relationship. Present only for everyone's entertainment.

Ray of Light- Madonna

KALEIDOSCOPIC OPTIMISM

Colors everywere, shapes the eye has never before seen, breath drawn in heavily, sweet smell of sea air.

Life is just as good as we are willing to make it. Beauty surrounds us. Cruelty, pain and negativity struggle to get in. Denied!

Dance circles around negative thoughts, people, situations. Create the life you dream of. No one is allowed in unless they apologize, bring flowers, and let go of any animosity past or present. There is no room for judgement.

Ride along with music playing and not a care in the world except to stand on a large cliff overlooking the sea with arms spread wide embracing triumph, gratitude and joy.

*This song reminds me of an optimistic person's innate ability to transcend all that is negative. Every time I hear it I am filled with joy.

Stranger in a Strange Land-Iron Maiden

ISOLATION

This theme consumes me. I am alone no matter who I am with. My life is like one long Twilight Zone episode.

Where is everybody?

Lonely.

Time Enough At Last.

A town with no people in it. A prisoner doomed to serve life without parole on a lonely asteroid. A selfish bibliophile who breaks his glasses right at the penultimate moment of his dream of reading uninterrupted.

For a family man solitude is sure something I overly crave. Why does a desolate landscape with no human interference except my own still intrigue me? I have come to the conclusion that not only am I misunderstood, I can't be understood.

I will remain a man without a country, without a home, no friends, no family. I have no need for such things. My heart is just as empty as the landscape, soul just as barren as the desert. I subsist in the eternal present. Breathing air. Moving forever forward.

*This song has always reminded me of resolute survival. That is, surviving for no particular reason. No path, no hope, just a blind desire to go on. An animal instinct to continue to exist.

Welcome to the Machine-Pink Floyd

INDUSTRIALLY SWALLOWED

A heavy sound pulses and is felt from all around. Natural things die and are replaced with motors, steel, and screws. Decay is not really possible because the world and everything in it is no longer alive. Just rust and things morphing into other things. Nothing is real.

An elevator descends and rapidly arrives in a mechanistic hell that looks all too familiar. This is the place that he has dreamt about for a very long time. It is deja-vu all over again. The first time he saw this place he was only a boy.

There was another place. The opposite destination. He knew it existed though he couldn't even picture it, he knew it was there because he could feel it. But he would never belong to the upper world. He was always destined for the down.

*This song always reminds me of a deep, mechanical hell that the acoustic guitar is trying to emerge from. The guitar represents humanity but in the end it gets swallowed by the dark beauty of the electric keyboards.

Miami 2017-Billy Joel

NOSTALGIA

The man knew good music. He listened to things far beyond what our teenage minds could comprehend. And we all loved it! But none of us had the courage to say so. We listened intently as we drove around in his car (he was the only one with a vehicle or a license) and sometimes caught each other mouthing the lyrics.

Such fearlessness in the face of ignorance. He knew what he liked, knew it was good, and didn't care what his uncompromising metalhead friends thought.

He was the first person to stick to his individuality while facing groupthink that I can recall.

I never got to tell him that he was really one of my first heroes.

*This song reminds me of Cai.

Skating Away On the Thin Ice of the New Day-Jethro Tull

MASTER OF THE EVERYDAY

Simplicity. Starting the day with a fresh cup of tea or coffee. Enjoying it thoroughly and without a hint of stress or rush. Nothing to be done or accomplished. The agenda is nonexistent.

You are free. You will do as you wish. You belong to no one. Nothing in particular has your attention. Yet the possibilities are unlimited.

The carnival that plays out in your head is building slowly and it is glorious. Piece by colorful piece the day takes shape, and you are glad you get to experience this.

To the uninitiated outsider it appears as if nothing much is happening but you know better. The joy of this simple miracle outweighs all. A new day fills your consciousness. You are well aware that many others have been denied this.

*This song has always represented simplicity, gratitude, and hope for me. It never fails to make me feel good when I hear it.

Simple.

Cruel Bloom-Converge

CARNY

Like every other new worker on the midway he started off with a heavy dose of optimism and fun. He considered it his duty to put a smile on the faces of all his transient patrons. Children, pretty ladies, couples, the elderly, none were exempt.

As time wore on something fundamental changed. He witnessed all who passed and began judging them with a more critical eye. Ungrateful kids, overly made-up harlots, disconnected couples, cynical old fogies that attempted to warn people that his game was a hoax.

Sadness crept in. Loneliness began to plague him. The carnival became his home as well as his prison. He had no way to alleviate this pain that had grown so strong within him. Once he had been a young man. Now he was a filthy middle aged shadow of his former self. Youth angered him, laughter saddened him, optimism enraged him. The game he had used to put a smile on people's faces had become nothing but a lure. A simple device to feed his nefarious and insatiable twisted desires. Patrons were now victims.

"Step right up folks. Try your luck!"

*This story was inspired by the idea of a carny worker watching his life pass him by and never establishing any roots. Observing life instead of living it. And in the end becoming a monster. The song Cruel Bloom by Converge is this individual's soundtrack as he completes his transformation from human being into something other.

Take the A Train-Duke Ellington

POSITIVITY

There is a distinct point in life, let's say a fork in the road where a choice must be made. Do I live miserably or happily? Do I allow myself to be beat down by life or do I dig deep and summon my natural resilience?

I admire those of us who make the positive choice. Bitterness and blame do not suit me. Being negative is a monumental waste of time, of life. It actually transforms you physically. Think Gollum and that "precious" ring.

Life is a painful rythym of meaningless moments or a powerful blast of joyful noise. Let that blast be loud baby!

Swing.

*This song always reminds me of happy meandering in NYC and all the possibilities of youth. Some music just fosters joy in the heart and Duke Ellington nailed it with this one.

In Your Words-Lamb of God

POWER PODIUM

A nameless politician mounts a stage in a small midwestern town. He waves briefly to the crowd assembled and steps behind the podium where he is transformed.

Suddenly he is bigger, better, somehow larger than life. The podium is what makes him begin to feel important. He is a legend in his own mind. A conqueror, a warrior, onstage to be worshipped by the masses. Resolute behind the podium. His wheel-less chariot and shield protecting him from equality and normalcy.

It is a wonder that he must play this game at all. He is fully prepared to be worshipped.

*This tune reminds me of what it would sound like if a politician finally decided to tell the truth from behind their podium. Being onstage and in the public eye is far more important to them than the actual issues. They do not represent the common man. And they believe themselves to be elite, above the law, untouchable, as well as special and somehow better than the average citizen.

Power has deluded their thinking. They need to be kept in check.

Who is doing this?

The only difference between the words politician and criminal are two other words:

Public Office.

Gimme Shelter-The Rolling Stones

SOMETHING'S COMING

Around every corner is an omen of some sort. People are losing hope. All of the hope and promise has faded. The happy carnival atmosphere has almost completely dissipated. Much of the planet is smoking, grey ruins. Yet still there is something worse on the way.

How could it get any worse you ask? Stop asking that question.

People are murdering each other for food. Mothers are killing their infants then going shopping with the tiny corpse in their oversized handbag. Religion has ceased to matter at all. Priests, monks, and nuns have all become predators like the rest.

No one listened to all of the predictions. The signs were all ignored. Something's coming. More will be revealed. Pay attention now. Eyes wide open. Batten down the hatches. Film at 11.

*This song always represents the end of the 60's for me. When the promise of a peaceful future was shot point blank in the head and murdered in front of the entire world.

Hole in the Sky-Black Sabbath w/Ozzy

RECKONING

The hole in the ozone.

Polar ice caps melting at a rapid rate.

Animals becoming extinct.

New global heat records being set each year.

Tsunamis.

Earthquakes.

Tornadoes.

Hurricanes.

The world is in obvious distress but we continue to consume as if "the rent's never due."

The lights will go out.

The day of reckoning will come.

Good luck to all.

Hug your loved ones.

Only the insane will survive.

The meek shall inherit the earth and all that happy horseshit.

Ready?

Too bad.

Here we go........

*This song somehow gives an optimistic, fuck it all, view of the apocalypse. Like; It's coming but until then Sabbath will continue to ROCK! Ozzy tells us we're all definitely fucked but we've been aware of this shit for years so fuck it.

Enjoy the final sunset bitches!

Round Midnight-Thelonious Monk

RAINY NYC STREETS

The rain drips from the awnings creating little puddles that run off into every gutter. A lone man in a brown raincoat walks and listens to the rainy night remembering many like it. Umbrellas shoot open, people run as if the raindrops were acid, vehicles splash through water-filled potholes and drench folks unfortunate enough to be standing at bus stops.

Street lights glisten off of wet surfaces. Stores and bars fluorescent colors shimmer in a million puddles. A melancholy permeates the wet city waiting for the sun to dry it away.

Jazz improvisations emerge from the semi-dark clubs and the man in the brown raincoat enters one and shakes himself off. He hangs his coat on the back of a high bar chair and heads toward the stage. It is still raining outside but he intends to produce a bit of sunshine from the piano bench to make these folks forget for a moment.

He looks at his right wrist and notices it is right around midnight.

Perfect.

*This song is a masterpiece that evokes exactly what I wrote above. All the promise of a Jazzman approaching his venue on a rainy night in NYC, Round Midnight.

Just a Bullet Away-Metallica

SONNY

She just said too much. Plain and simple she never shut the fuck up. Opinions on this, ideas about that, how his and everyone else' life should be lived. He was tired. Exhausted in fact. Did he have the courage to do it?

BLAM! Shit, it wasn't her but it was the next best thing.

Night after hot summer night he shot someone else. He really wanted this bitch dead but he hadn't been able to yet. He was afraid of her. She was fucking scary.

Then one night he decided that enough innocents had died. He carefully cleaned and polished his .45, waited until she slept and shot her shrew fucking face off through her grandmother's ugly ass throw pillow. He cut her up nice and disposed of the pieces and the blasted pillow in a dumpster in Pelham.

When the pigs finally picked him up for the other murders the bitch was never mentioned.

It's been years now. He has told everyone he's been saved by Jesus Christ. But in the dead of night amidst the scattered screams and crying in the cellblock he has his private fantasy. The bitch's body picked clean by seagulls and turkey vultures on top of the giant landfill in Staten Island, until she was literally just a screaming skeleton. In the name of the father, son, and holy ghost you fucking bitch.

*This song reminds me of the Son of Sam/David Berkowitz. Jesus my ass!!!

Egg Man-Beastie Boys

SUMMER MISSIONS

It started as a humid scorcher melting with pure boredom, sneaker bottoms sticking to the hot pavement.

At least ten ideas of what to do shot down and complained about.

Anger and frustration set in like a natural by-product of the summer heat.

What to do?

Where to go?

Who to see?

Finally a decision is made on how to successfully waste another 24 hour summer day.

The idea is stupid.

Dangerous.

Delinquent.

People get hurt.

Chaos occurs.

Nobody gets caught. Tomorrow is supposed to be even hotter.

*This song reminds me of chaotic youth. How in the hell did we always decide to cause trouble? There were many choices but trouble always seemed to win out. Fucking delinquents.

Fight the Power-Public Enemy

STAND UP

Everything and everyone should be questioned. And the number one question should be:

Why do you believe you have dominion over me?

This patriarchal, hierarchical society created by the rich, white, minority is done. It cannot continue.

Politicians should be handed shovels to dig us out from under their bullshit and lies. Police and judges should be handed public beatings by those they have railroaded.

Every boss should be removed from their offices and escorted to the factory floor, straight to the front lines, back to the fucking trenches. What made them believe that their leadership was needed?

Side by side, not the stupid human pyramid. We are all equal whether you like it or not. The rest is just illusions, nonsense and smokescreens.

Get up, stand up, and fight the fucking power. We are the majority. What are we waiting for?

Burn this mother down!!!

*Obviously this song has always been an anthem. A rallying cry for the fed up and disposessed everywhere.

Eminence Front-The Who

REGRETFUL LOOK BACK

Why didn't I live more? Tomorrow never came. I always said I'd get to it later and before long I was 50. 50! I never thought I'd live this long truth be told. I thought I would've cashed out way before prostate exams and colonoscopy's.

Did I love enough?

Give enough?

Was I kind enough? Notice, I didn't ask the question: Do I have enough? Because now it doesn't matter. Whatever was important had to do with the heart not the wallet.

My wallet is still empty despite the constant pursuit of money. My soul has holes in it and my heart is dust. I didn't learn a thing. I collected knowledge but never internalized it. I was a dilletante of the worst sort.

I'm not dying. But if something doesn't happen real soon I've wasted this gift. Christ, I never even unwrapped it.

Is it too late?

*This song reminds me of a person looking back at his days with disgust and dissatisfaction. He traipses throughout his house hitting and breaking things. Did he waste it all? Does he have enough time to change or will he call it a day? You be the judge.

Last Goodbye-Jeff Buckley

RELUCTANT COMPLETION

He did not feel worthy to go forward with this relationship. But he was joyful nevertheless. She had given him light and unconditional love, however brief. Although he was only human and things would sadden him when he remembered, he knew this was a liaison that would never be rekindled. It was over. Completely and forever.

The next time he felt love it would be different, stronger, devoid of selfishness. But it was because of this relationship that he would be able to recognize this.

For this realization he was forced to remain grateful to her. He supposed he would always love her for that. Strange. Funny how life and especially love works.

*This song always reminds me of the joy discoverable within the sadness of a dying relationship. Humans are always capable of moving on. That is if they give themselves time. New adventures constantly await.

Fuck You-Cee Lo Green

THE TRUE GOODBYE

There are many who "got away". Different types of women who for one reason or another just could not hang. Apparently everything was always all my fault or so I've been told. The logic is that I was the common denominator in all of these doomed relationships. Well I say, Fuck that.

It's not that any of these bitches were batshit crazy as hell perhaps? Or that they had such deep seated issues that they were going to make me pay for all of them? Or, wait for it.....

.....they would never, ever, be satisfied no matter how many sacrifices were made because something in them was lacking.

Well, this is the real, true goodbye for all of you. I'm letting every single one of your ungrateful skeletons out of my closet once and for all. Erasing your memories from my skull. Funny thing is, now you know the kind of love I gave you. You're regretful because you never found that kind of emotion again no matter how hard you tried.

Yes. I loved you completely. Unconditionally. With my whole heart. But you didn't want it. You didn't want me. But you do now.

Well, I recovered from all of your lack of gratitude, neglect, and witholding natures. My broken heart healed. And when it did she was standing right there.

Waiting.

*I love this song. The ultimate kiss off. Set to hopeful, uplifting music. This is for every man that ever gave everything and got absolutely nothing in return.

A Day In The Life-The Beatles

PROPHECY

We're all just living. Some wasting their precious moments on this planet and others taking advantage of their time. But one thing is certain, we're all looking to fill our lives with something.

Some choose pain, addiction, anger and pettiness. Others health, beauty, travel and money. The curious thing about it is that we all have both sides within us.

Does any of it really matter? We like to think it does. We like to believe that our lives have meaning. But do they really? Will any of us truly matter in the end? Go ahead, shout loudly into the abyss that you matter. I have a sneaky suspicion that I don't. But it doesn't stop me from going to work everyday and doing what must be done.

As a matter of fact, I have to go.

I'm already terribly late.

*Quite simply a masterpiece. This song came out in 1967 the year of my birth. My parents had a copy of Sgt. Pepper's and they often played it. The album disturbed me somewhere down deep. Especially this tune. It evoked a whole range of emotions that I could never express until now at the age of 47 with the humble piece above. Oh, and I almost forgot. At the end of my days I am sure I will hear that haunting, sustained piano chord. A fitting end to a life begun in the same year that A Day In The Life appeared on the scene. Make sure they play that shit at my funeral!!!

Centerpiece-Sonata Allegro

Many styles and various forms of music resound throughout a typical life. These Miniature Symphonies are some of the pieces that make up the soundtrack of my existence. I could not imagine living without music. In fact, the mere prospect of that remote possibility is nothing less than terrifying. I am a person who literally needs music. Music is one of those beautiful gifts from the Creator. An absolute joy to be marveled at and pondered over within the deepest levels of mind, heart, body, and

soul.

Many pieces of music were studied and listened to during the creation of this book. Music from different cultures, different eras, different parts of the globe. Each form was unequivocally embraced and listened to without prejudice, as all music should be. No need to judge. Just enjoy.

This work could never contain all of the bands, composers, songs, and musicians that have influenced me. If that were the case this book would not be just one volume. It would contain several and perhaps be my life's work.

No. This book is to offer up the idea of inspiration and how close writing, music, and film can be. How closely they are related, even interrelated. Think about how some films would not exist if the director had not heard a particular song and imagined the scene it would fit perfectly with. It is hard to imagine Steinbeck or Bukowski's work without the influence of classical music.

Music, it is said, is the purest of all art forms. It can evoke a feeling quicker than a photo, painting, film, or string of words. Music is the common denominator for all artistic endeavor. From music flows all creativity and music must continue to exist in order to unite all people artistic or otherwise. Music is the universal language. If you wish to discover where a person is coming from ask them: "What kind of music do you listen to?"

The pieces in this book were inspired by the written word, films, but above all music. I would venture to guess that I would not be a writer without music. Nor a husband, father, or productive human being.

Music is as important to me as breathing. It is that fundamental to my survival.

For those of you who have been affected by music in such a manner you already understand. No explanation necessary. For you folks that can't fathom what it is I'm going on about I pray that this book opens your eyes and introduces you to the wonderful gift of music.

Do not judge.

Do not complain.

Just forge ahead.

Open your mind, your ears and of course your heart and enjoy the rest of the show.

Listen.

SECTION 2:

RESIST CATEGORIZATION

The following are the albums I lived with and listened to for inspiration leading into this second section:

1. James Brown-20 All Time Greatest Hits!

   The Godfather of Soul is a pure entertainer. He can dance, sing, and as bandleader he is unrivaled. When I hear him my feet begin to move. And folks, I do not dance!

2. Talib Kweli-The Beautiful Struggle

   This album is an urban masterpiece. Kweli is an independent MC that gets down to it and makes you feel. When I was running a meditation/music appreciation group in a youth rehab in the early 2000's many a stressed out teen bobbed their heads to this one and momentarily forgot their problems. While being simultaneously inspired.

3. Ray LaMontagne-Til the Sun Turns Black

   A relatively new discovery for me. LaMontagne is a singer songwriter loaded with talent. Beautiful melancholia.

4. Owl City-Ocean Eyes

   A suggestion from my daughter Roxanne. A happy mix of real instruments and electronic sounds. Ironic lyrics sang in a lilting hipster voice stolen directly from Blink-182. Happy though. And likable. Optimism as music.

5. U2-All That You Can't Leave Behind

   An album full of hope and freedom. Particularly the track "Walk On". An anthem to the power of resilience. This song gives me chills every time I hear it.

6. Walter Trout-Unspoiled By Progress

Trout, an inveterate road dog ripping it up with his brand of smokin' electric blues. He sometimes makes folks like Clapton look as though they are standing still while playing.

During my bartending career Egon (one of the owners of Ramapo Valley Brewery) booked Trout to play on a Sunday night. The place was far from packed but from my vantage point behind the bar I witnessed one of the greatest blues guitarists of all time light the place on fire. I had no idea who he was until that day but my jaw as well as everyone else's hit the floor when he began playing. Old Walter destroyed that joint as if it were Carnegie Hall. The mark of a true performer. No matter how small the venue, or how many people are there, play like your life depends on it. Walter Fuckin' Trout does it every time.

7. Fiona Apple-When the Pawn...

Ominous awareness is how I would classify Fiona Apple's work. She is painfully aware of the power she posesses as a musician and a vocalist. Her piano playing punches you hard in the stomach and her voice wrings out your heart as if it were a bloodsoaked sponge.

8. Eminem-The Eminem Show

An absolutely incredible rhymer. A master of inventive outsized violent wordplay. I've always been impressed with his facility with the language. Every time I listen to him I always wind up shaking my head and smiling.

9. Black Sabbath-Sabotage

Sabotage always struck me as an ethereal record. Ozzy howling away untethered about to lose his mind and everything else.

10. King Diamond-The Eye

King Diamond's mad treatise on the idea of witch trials and mini-inquisitions. Heavy on riffage and synthesizers as well as the King's angry falsetto.

11. Heart- Greatest Hits

Deep grooves. Awesome vocals. Hyper catchy memorable arrangements. Songs that run the gamut of human emotion. They made it ok for women to rock and for men to appreciate them.

12. Guns & Roses-Chinese Democracy

Universally panned as not worth waiting for. It took Axl a billion years to produce this piece of garbage? But somehow I love this shit. Some of the songs stay with you and Axl destroys his voice to bring you this record. Shitty as it may be, it's honest.

13. Papa Roach-Infest

Behind the bar at Mugg's Pub in 2000. A totally usual night of serving underage college kids and maybe even a handful of high schoolers. A short, spiky haired dude with tattoos and his pal belly up and marvel at the amount of pretty girls there are. The dude was Coby Dick of Papa Roach. I had no idea who he was or that his band was on the verge of stardom. All I know is that he and his buddy were gentlemen both leaving a 20 dollar tip apiece. Later I saw the video for Last Resort and recognized them. Thanks boys!

14. Moby-Play

The year was 1999. It was before the devastation of 9/11/01 and the dissolution of my first marriage. I still had some innocence left. And I was still very, very drunk. This record brings it all back.

15.Beastie Boys-Paul's Boutique

A great record all the way through and around. It always brings a smile to my face. During my stint at the youth rehab I played it regularly for the kids. One day I forgot to review what I was playing and in the giant space of the rec room the unmistakeable sound of someone hitting a water bong echoed out into the hallway. Shit! I thought. I forgot that was on there! Every kid's head turned simultaneously and they all laughed. After all, the green was what most of them were there for. Even the clinical director who was walking by out in the hallway at that exact moment knew something was up. She couldn't quite put her finger on it, but that loud bubbling sound was rather suspicious.

16. Bach-Six Unaccompanied Cello Suites

These suites are unbearably beautiful. They transport me to another time and place. The Cello is an incredible instrument. It 'almost' rivals the bagpipes for spine chilling capabilities. It is hard to believe that Bach was once ignored. He vowed to produce so much music it would be impossible to continue to ignore him. He succeeded.

17. The Beatles-The White Album

This album was always in heavy rotation at my Aunt's house when I was little. I liked it. It made me feel weird, sort of in a dream. Words like sad, angry, depressed came much later. I prefer to listen with my child's mind. Yes. The Beatles are better understood by children.

18. Jane's Addiction-Ritual de lo Habitual

An ethereal masterpiece. Listen to this entire album. Not just "Been Caught Stealing". Although Dave Navarro's guitar work on that song is massive and otherworldly. Perry Farrell's voice is absolutely haunting. Perfection.

19. INXS-Kick

I always thought INXS had far more potential than they were allowing themselves. Although they did attain pop stardom due largely to MTV, VH1 and their crossover appeal, they could've been more. Unfortunately that bar would never be hurdled. It was prevented by a thin snakeskin belt and massive depression.

20. Miles Davis-Greatest Hits

Miles was and still is an enigma. His music was and is among the most inventive in any genre. He was a composer and arranger of enormous depth and creativity. He knew just how to create the right mood. I saw Miles live in New York City at the Pier with John McLaughlin. I wasn't fully aware of what he was pulling off but my musically well rounded heavy metal bandmates were all astounded. Their mouths remained agape for most of the performance and they punched me on the arm or slapped me on the back out of pure joy after Miles soloed wildly or achieved some musical miracle.

21. Black Sabbath-Vol. 4

An album known about but discovered relatively late. An absolute tour de force. Sabbath at the top of their game. The musicianship on this record is incredible. Henry Rollins was right when he said that this one was their best. I agree.

22. Rob Zombie-The Sinister Urge

Rob Zombie is a striking figure. He is a post-apocalyptic vision of what this culture with it's monsters and ultra-violent images has done to us. His music is a metallic industrial punch in the teeth.

23. The Doors-Waiting for the Sun

First off, I stole this cassette from the local 5 and dime when I was 12 years old. This is the first time I am telling anyone. This entire album represents guilt and the outlaw for me. It was the first thing I ever stole. I'll never forget the heart-pounding adrenaline rush while walking past the cashier. Or the thrill of having succeeded. Then going home and hearing "Not to Touch the Earth" and thinking that these guys wrote this song especially for me and I was now the Lizard King and I could do anything.

24.Guns -n- Roses-Appetite for Destruction

This album was released when I was 2 years out of high school. It was grittier than the rest of the hair metal coming out of the 80's. A sharp return to heavy rock with a groove. But somehow it offered hope. Hope with an edge. But hope nevertheless. Listen to Paradise City, I can't really explain what I mean but that song embodies what I'm trying to say.

25. David Bowie-Earthling

Bowie is a genius. He has reinvented himself more times than a chameleon. Musically he is hyper-creative. When you think about his output it is nothing short of astounding. Bowie has been making music for 5 decades! "I'm Afraid of Americans" is a favorite track off of this album.

26. ZZ Top-Greatest Hits

I love ZZ Top. There's probably not a song of theirs I don't enjoy. Apart from the space hillbilly image they cultivated in the 80's I even love their look. Those beards are iconic. The song "Tush" is my all time favorite though. There is a mysterious power to that song. And there isn't a single time I have listened to it that I hadn't wished it was longer. The song is too short!

27. Neil Young-Psychedelic Pill

This record with Crazy Horse gets better, richer, every time I hear it. It's like they found that old groove and just jammed on it for an entire album. Young's guitar playing is great on this one. Listen to "Walk Like a Giant". When I was much younger I was in a short lived classic rock band and we covered "Cortez the Killer". A beast of a song and still my favorite Neil Young tune. Psychedelic Pill is a return to this long form sensibility.

28. Common-Be

This record is a lyrical bomb. It made me realize what hip hop could be. I defy anyone to keep from bobbing their head throughout this album. Common reaches down deep within his culture and experience and really makes you realize what it means to struggle. If you have not really struggled you will not understand this.

29. Beastie Boys-Ill Communication

A great mix of punk, hip hop, and experimental music. The boys got inventive on this record. They rapped ferociously and played their own instruments finding grooves in both ways, as well as using many different studio tricks and innovative techniques. This album is a staple wherever I am.

30. Ramones- Ramonesmania

The Ramones were a force of nature. A driving barrage of 2 to 3 minute gems that always left you wanting more. Power chords, highhat bashing, and Joey's mouth full of marshmallows vocals belting out retro surf and rockabilly shlock. There is a picture of Joey Ramone floating around on the internet. It's a black and white of Joey at the mic. It reads:

"Sometimes I get sad that Joey Ramone is dead. Then I get happy that Joey Ramone lived."

Indeed.

31. Sting-Ten Summoner's Tales

I always considered Sting to be a great talent. Musician, vocalist, songwriter, bandleader etc. This is one of my favorite records of his. His storytelling is hard to match in terms of the journey his music takes you on. He takes you and you go willingly. I was in Europe when this record was released and I needed some hope and strength to carry me through some rough times. Sting provided a much needed musical refuge. I still possess the very same copy from 1992.

32. Television-Marquee Moon

I came to them late but Television is one of my favorite bands. I was a bit too young for them because I came of age in the 80's but if I had been exposed to them I would have surely fallen in love. Tom Verlaine and the boys came out of that 70's New York post punk scene and never allowed themselves to be co-opted by the establishment. They packed it in before that could happen. Short lived but beautiful, powerful work.

33. Tim Buckley-Starsailor

People thought he lost his mind when he made this album. That's probably why I enjoy it. Buckley departed completely from the tried and true folk formula he had been using with conventional arrangements, good guitar playing and beautiful vocals. He flew way out there with experimental vocals, arrangements, instruments etc. He had absolutely no regard for his audience and he destroyed commerciality entirely. He was a pioneer. A maverick. A true musician. Testing the limits of sound and his own wild voice.

34. Jeff Buckley-Grace

A haunting work of art. The first time I played the record all the way through I was astounded by how good this guy's voice was. The first 3 tracks; Mojo Pin, Grace, and Last Goodbye floored me. But the album is a mysterious whole. Every track transcendent in its own way. Hope, joy, love, pain, loss, it's all in there. Perhaps he knew this would be the only one he would complete. What an incredible talent was lost the night Jeff Buckley drowned in the Mississippi river. But he left us with a bonafide masterpiece.

35. AC/DC-Black Ice

A great piece of rock and roll mayhem. Hearkening back to their other black album the illustrious Back In Black. Angus is in excellent form as well as the rest of the band. Brian Johnson is at his glass gargling best. I would've thought this dude's vocal chords would be entirely shredded 30+ years on. I would've been wrong.

36. Fiona Apple-Extraordinary Machine

Apple has graduated from cute, cherubic, dangerous youth to a full-fledged bad woman with an arsenal of songwriting and instrument playing weapons. When I listen to her I sense menace underneath her playful lyrics. She beats and bangs the piano hard enough to make Bukowski very proud.

37. The Flaming Lips-Embryonic

The Lips are all experimental all the time. This record reminds me of something Floyd would have arrived at had Syd Barrett remained at the helm and been given the technology along with free reign.

38. Queensryche-Here In the Now Frontier

Geoff Tate's voice is an instrument that sends shivers down the spine. The dual guitar attack of Chris DeGarmo and Michael Wilton as well as all of the other musicians involved makes for one of the tightest bands to ever pick up instruments. When I listen to this record I notice the groove and I'm carried away. Queensryche has always been good to listen to in the car while driving. Fast.

39. Living Colour-Stain

I've been a fan of this band since day one. Something about their connectedness as a group. Socially conscious lyrics backed by heavy grooves and beastly guitar work. And rythym baby. Stevie Wonder has a similar effect on me with heavier tunes like Superstition and Higher Ground. I came across this album while still in Europe and was blown away.
Still am.

40. Highway 61 Revisited-Bob Dylan

As will probably always be the case Dylan is an enigma. This record pisses me off somehow. Perhaps I am jealous of his storytelling facility or how he seems oblivious to how his music affects people. Dylan's music is joyous and suicide inducing all at once. Yeah. That's it. Dylan's entire catalogue is one long heartfelt suicide note for civilization as we know it. He's saying goodbye for all of us. And he's not at all happy about being the number one doomsayer. But he continues to do it. And he began telling us with this record. He warned us. But of course, we didn't listen.
We never really do.

BOOKS

LIZARD KING

Born into discipline and structure. In his world there was a place and a time for everything. Spontaneity was a bad word. Inventiveness was frowned upon. Play was viewed with suspicion.

He began to grow, as children will do. This life began to chafe. He was questioning everything. By 17 it no longer suited him. So he left. His father laughed at him. He shot his father in the face.

The open road welcomed him. He stayed on it for a long time. Traversing the continent grew tiring so he headed west. Because maybe just maybe the west was the best.

Over time he transformed himself into the Lizard King. He held generations of young ones enthralled. It was his destiny. That singular destiny led him to die in a beautiful clawfoot Parisian bathtub of a massive heart attack brought on by a Heroin overdose.

He was a creative soul. A poet of the first order and coming into his own artistically after years of being misunderstood.

His body lies with other great artists, writers, and poets in Pere Lachaise cemetery in Paris, France. Generations of fools visit every year and miss the point entirely. A cautionary tale would be totally lost on them as they piss and pour beer over his final resting place.

He was the Lizard King now he can't do a fucking thing.

Because he's dead.

*Whoever stole the bust of Jim Morrison from Pere Lachaise, please put it back. Have some fucking respect. And stop with the graffiti and defacing of other people's tombs. Morrison would be mortified by this behavior fuckers! I have already read the majority of his stuff and find it very dense and atmospheric like all great writing should be.

I almost suffered the same fate. But I put the shit down and started writing. I'm still writing for my life. Morrison should have written for his.

NOW I AM THE FUCKING LIZARD KING!!!

And I have done everything! Except . . .

. . . die of an overdose.

It took me so many years to realize what a fucking waste that 27 club is. So much artistry and talent extinguished needlessly.

Rest in Peace knuckleheads.

CEMENT

His face bounces off the macadam. He feels blood pouring from his nose. A boot smashes his bloody cheek shattering it entirely. He feels two large hands on the back of his head. Gingerly they guide his head towards the curb. He can feel his mouth opening, then his teeth and tongue taste gritty concrete. Suddenly there is no more light. None. It remains completely dark.

How does he feel about what he's done? There is no feeling except hatred. Hate is all that remains. Hate, pure as the driven snow. The vicious, violent act he just performed was a by product of hate. Hate. Pure, rocklike, firebranded into his consciousness. A beacon to follow.

The next individual to fuck with him will always regret it. He is a child of violence. But there is always another way.

*A spellbinding book about the murder of Rollins' best friend right in front of him. Joe Cole is memorialized in this book. Rollins elegantly describes how losing a friend in such a manner can cause unbelievable pain and serious amounts of prodigious hate. All channeled into some incredible form of performance that still remains unmatched. Positive from negative. Light from dark. But the sadness and bloodstains remain.

THE DEVIL'S INTERVAL

The flatted fifth bewitched her. When he played it for her she felt frissons ride up and down her spine. Like the dark one himself had just set foot in the room. It scared her down deep, but once he began she didn't want him to stop.

Then came the fateful day that she always knew would come. The mob arrived screaming, shouting, for their heads and they meant to have them. They would settle for nothing less than blood.

She was tied tightly to him. His lute in between. Their throats were slashed open and they were lit ablaze by torches.

As she sat in agony bleeding out and burning alive she could hear the unmistakeable rattle of the devil's interval getting louder by the second. The floor opened up beneath them and the mob was swallowed up, every last one of them. Her bleeding stopped, her skin was doused with a gentle breeze and stopped burning.

Her lover was gone. Charred beyond recognition. But the lute remained intact.

When she played her fury was palpable. No one ever bothered her again.

Ever.

*This work was dense. Hard to penetrate. Harder to enjoy. But several passages induced deep thought and made me realize that not every subject was made to be philosophized about. Some topics are better left a mystery.

This House On Fire: The Story of the Blues by Craig Awmiller

THE GRIOT

He was fierce. And he knew it. One of the best players that had ever slid his fingers along a fretboard. But there was something missing. Like there was an invisible key that would finally unlock the hidden door.

He played for folks everywhere he could. They seemed to enjoy it but he never could get onto a big stage in a classy joint.

Yeah he'd heard of the crossroads but the devil wasn't getting his soul. He had plans for that little piece of beauty. Besides, he needed it to play. So he worked harder than any bluesman alive. Night after night, dive after dive, he shredded until his brow sweat and fingers bled.

There were many who seemingly surpassed him. But in the end he won. He had legions of loyal fans and his soul was his own and preparing to fly. His was a Satisfied Mind.

*This book was a great introduction to the blues. A short, concise, yet impactful little piece of work. I like books that pack a punch without an overabundance of useless atmospherics. If I want details and description I'll put the book down and go see for myself.

Hot Water Music-Charles Bukowski

SURVIVAL OF THE SHITTIEST

Acrid smoke fills the air of a filthy, bottle strewn, hotel room. When he gets up he pulls at the ass of his damp boxers and kicks a few empties out of his path on the way to the shitter. He burps loudly, hocks a loogey in the sink, then vomits in the tub before releasing the nastiest shit imaginable into the severely stained toilet.

Later, when he is brushing his few remaining teeth he retches at his own lingering stench. He only gets dressed to go out and buy more liquor or to pick up a cheap booze whore.

His entire existence is about satisfying his various cravings. There is no good reason for him to live. But he will live. Until the ripe old age of 83.

Across town a 12 year old girl prays for God to let her live, for the pain to stop, and for her grandfather to stay sober long enough to come visit her.

*Bukowski has always been one of my favorites. He is above all a fantastic read. Whatever he writes seems interesting. No matter what the subject.

However, he always reminds me of the angry, ungrateful slob. You know, the decrepit old fuck that survives everything while innocent children die in agony. The piece of shit who constantly laments his awful plight while the sweet little disease ridden toddler smiles through bleeding chemo-ravaged gums.

Ghost Rider: Travels On the Healing Road

THE SURFACE OF AN ANCIENT ICEFIELD

Loss hits like a bomb. It shatters everything in an instant. You are shaken i every bone. Every part of you hurts. If the loss is great enough there is almost nothing of you left.

You're like a broken ghost standing alone on the surface of an ancient icefield in a land decimated by cold. Movement seems to be the only remedy. Continuous movement. When you're moving you're safe from memory. A sort of untouchable target. There must be a moment of reckoning. A scar before it heals is called a wound. You need to feel pain in order to scar.

Stop.

Feel.

Heal.

It is amazing how the human organism survives. This sort of sorrow is not natural. It is almost too much to bear.

But it's not.

There's more to do.

So you live on.

For now.

Until the next catastrophe?

*Neil Peart lost his 19 year old daughter to a car accident and his wife to cancer in the same year. This book was about his healing process. This piece is for the memory of his wife and daughter.

Enough said.

RENAISSANCE LIFE

Music is everywhere. It is necessary to play it. Listening is not enough. Drawing on cocktail napkins relentlessly between gigs. Napkins are not enough. Sketching in notebooks every spare moment. Sketching is not enough.

He picked up a paintbrush. Canvases were produced and there was satisfaction at first. But he needed his subjects to move. Filming became the medium of choice. He put together beautiful works. Not films per se. Intense collections of images that transcended story and conventional narrative so much so that they were no longer needed as a guide and people just filled in the blanks and began to think for themselves. However, for him it was not enough.

When he began writing something within him clicked. A cosmic domino fell. He knew this was it. It was finally enough. He had found his artistic home.

*Rivers was not only a genius at art. He was a master at life. He spent much of his life poor. Destitute even. But it never stopped his journey into art. He had to work. There was no other way. People had to let him. Rivers made his entire life a work of art. He was an interesting man. I found the book years ago in a rustic independent bookstore named Pickwick in Nyack, New York.

Dream Brother-The Lives of Tim and Jeff Buckley by David Browne

SATISFIED SADNESS

A father has a son. The father leaves. It's not natural. The father is supposed to have patience and wait until the son leaves. When the natural cycle is defied someone always pays.

The father dies and leaves a second time. His son pays dearly for his father's selfishness. He misses his father so much his entire life is spent hurtling headlong towards death. The only possible means to reunite with him.

Though he is not fully aware of this, the son checks out early in a drowning accident. I sincerely hope he found his Dad at the end of his painful journey. And his Dad apologized to him for his thoughtlessness.

*This book was well written and informative. But I believe Jeff Buckley would have rolled over in his grave had he seen the clever structure of the book. A chapter on his father, then a chapter on him. This juxtaposition seemed intrusive and unnecessary. Like their lives weren't their own. Each person merited a book of their own. And knowing how Jeff felt about his father in life should have been respected. He was a better musician and a better man. And I suspect if he had lived to have children he would've been a better father than his own.

Bumping Into Geniuses-My Life Inside the Rock and Roll
Business by Danny Goldberg

RIGHT PLACE FOR A GRAND ADVENTURE

Every day he swept up, rolled cords, emptied ashtrays, got
those motherfuckers coffee and booze or something to eat if
they wanted. They thought he was their own personal errand
boy. Son of a bitch, he hated this shit!

Then one day it happened. He was mopping out one of the
toilets and he heard a particular playback blasting over the
studio soundsystem. It sounded like shit. But suddenly he knew
exactly what would make it sound better. He sprinted down the
hallway and forced his way into the booth.

The rest, as they say, is history. He just happened to be at
the right place at the right time. Or was it that he always suited
up and showed up, worked his ass off and didn't quit when the
going got tough?

Whatever it was his career was a long one. And no matter
how many people he worked with he made sure to appreciate
every one. Especially the studio bitch, because that had been
him. And deep down he knew it could be him again.

*I loved Goldberg's book and despite his meteoric rise through
the ranks of the record business he seemed like a down to earth
cat. Bravo Danny for hanging on to your soul when others in
your position have sold theirs or simply just lost it.

FILMS

Kevin

COMEBACK KID

Something is not quite right. It's all there. The talent, the drive, the material. He is even original in a sea of imitators. But there is a huge, unseen obstacle. It crushes with its imposing weight. It tries to make him believe he is already at his destination, when the road is actually much longer. Hubris. Pride. A fucking head the size of Long Island.

He moves to what he believes is the launching point. The place is better suited to spread his unique brand of musical originality. His home spot doesn't quite get it. He has a desire to be understood widely. He knows he has it in him to communicate globally. He is full of beautiful music.

On a normal night in this new place he is faced with a confrontation. A moment of truth. The music gets shocked and beaten out of him. The dream flickers, gutters like an almost dying candle flame.

For years he does not play. The instrument stays silent, the dream lays dormant. Regular work. 9 to 5 routine and family pain. He ponders how people can inflict and survive pain while rebuilding his body and mind.

Then a chance encounter with a person who he affected years before with his music. A journey to where it all began and his true life and music relaunched.

*The film Kevin is a message of hope for all artists who thought it was over and the window had closed. As long as we breathe it's not over.

Create.

 Believe.

Come back.

 Kevin Gant did.

DAD ARTISTRY

A giant middle finger to the establishment. A rebellious fuck you shouted out for all to hear and ponder over. Never succumb. Never surrender.

Daddy! I wanna play with you!

Shit. That's right I'm a father. When the fuck did this happen? Almost 24 years ago. And yet I'm still who I am. Still the first guy to question authority and call people out on their bullshit.

But I have more than one child now. My baby girl just called me and wants to play right now. Right this second. Do I rebel against her? Do I tell her no?

Daddy! I hear all of my children say over the years. I have been here for all of them. My kids are more important than any form of rebellion, any anti-political statement or any artistic endeavor. My children and being a father is the most important thing I will ever do. A father is the most important thing I will ever be.

Kids, your Daddy loves you. More than you will ever know.

Maybe I made some mistakes along the way. Especially when I was young and stupid, but rest assured all of you, the second you came into my life you were never out of my thoughts.

Fatherhood is my true passion. You are all my works of art.

*I loved this film. It made me realize many things. The most important that being a writer is secondary to being a father. But my writing is informed by my fatherhood and vice versa. I certainly would not be the person I am without the love of my children. I would be a lesser man.

The Making of Sacrament-Lamb of God

GREETINGS FROM THE HEAVY

Rehearse, rehearse, rehearse. Practice, practice, practice. That's what must be done if you want to be successful. That's what it means to be heavy. Others think you just get this way. No. With a capital N. This shit takes discipline.

If you are not willing to sacrifice for this, to sweat and bleed and suffer then go do something else because you're just playing. You cannot play if you want this. You must work.

The fun comes after the brutal, slogging, painful work. That's the release point. And you can only attain full release after the pain. There will be other small moments but if you don't put the work in they pale in comparison.

I bid you greetings from the Heavy. Only Warriors need apply.

*Lamb of God is a hardworking metal band. They understand the value of hard work and how it translates to their success. This film is inspirational because of that fact.

Hard Work + Discipline = Success

For musicians there is no other equation. Especially in the beginning. Otherwise your band is just a hobby.

Who Is Harry Nilsson?

FAMILY MAN

It's tragic when an unapologetic life becomes somewhat apologetic out of necessity.

He was a monster of a singer songwriter. Whipping out material at a prodigious rate. Living just as fast as the music was coming. Then later he found the love of his life and had a couple of children. His former way of doing things did not suit fatherhood. Unfortunately it was too late for him to change. The lifestyle had seeped deep into his bones. But he did his level best.

He loved his children. His wife. His family and friends. He felt his pain and their needs deeply. But the monster had him, and it wasn't letting go. "Make the most of it," became his motto.

He did.

*This film was an excellent look into the end of the 60's into the excess of the 70's and 80's, and the struggle of a man discovering fatherhood a bit too late. At the end of the film when Nilsson is in failing health you root for him to recover so he can be with his beloved family.

But the music.

Extraordinary.

 An underrated genius.

Stranger:

Bernie Worrell On Earth

AN ORIGINAL OPUS

He played in order to communicate. There was no other option for him. For some reason other avenues were entirely closed off. So he played. And he played. And he played some more.

He never really practiced per se. Sure he learned scales, how to read, and all of that didactic shit, but only long enough to break the rules and re-invent.

Day after day he slammed away never realizing that he was in flux. He was in a cocoon waiting to emerge as a butterfly. In order to write a masterpiece you must be a master first.

He wrote and played nonstop his entire life always trying to create that one particular piece that he would be remembered for. What he failed to realize was that he was the original opus. His body, his mind, his spirit. Without him his music did and would not exist. The recordings paled in comparison to the live event. You could not divorce the man from his music. Only he could play it.

When he finally understood he began to play with more passion and abandon than ever before. Yes, he was remembered. He left recordings behind when he died. But his essence could not be pinned down. All of it went with him. Memories and recorded music are all we have. That's why there is sadness. Because it will never be the same again.

*Bernie Worrell is quite simply a beast. Everything he does should be applauded and appreciated before he leaves this life. This film was a fine tribute to his originality and refusal to succumb to the usual trappings of being a working musician. He focused entirely on the music.

Entirely.

Metallica-Through the Never

THE MYSTERIOUS SATCHEL

Something is in that bag. I don't know what the hell it is. But everyone wants it.

Everyone.

What could it be? Not enough time to find out. Not enough time to care. It's taken on a life of it's own. At this point even if the satchel is empty it does not matter.

Chase that piece of cloth with a zipper. Chase it unto the ends of the earth. Nothing and no one can stop me. I now have the ultimate piece of the puzzle. The one piece that everyone wants, everyone desires.   Purpose.

No why's. No what for's. Just pure mission. Pure purpose. Funny that it's a fucking bag. Just a little fucking cloth satchel. Who the hell would've thought? Life boiled down to its lowest common denominator. Get it, because I want it. I need it. Gotta have it.

I will get it.

There's no other way.

Here I go.

To hell and back motherfuckers!

*Metallica never really disappoints me. I am a fan for sure. A great admirer. This film is awesome because there is no explanation. The band and filmmakers let the viewer make up their own mind.

That's freedom.

That's what I strive to do with my writing.

Think for your fucking self! You have a mind.

Use it.

Mo' Better Blues

WHAT GOES AROUND

All the Jazz in the world can't fill an empty heart. But there are those that have made the choice. Everything else is secondary to the music.

Miles, Coltrane, Bird, there are many bitten by that bug. Still others will be. Perhaps that is why their music remains so important. It was literally all they had. Everything else paled in comparison.

Tragedy, Beauty, Love, Loss, Sacrifice. They put it all into their music. And music was life.

*Mo' Better Blues was one of those films for me. What happens when you allow music to take over your life? Then what happens if you lose your music or the ability to play? This great film attempts to answer these and other questions.

Ghost Blues-The Story of Rory Gallagher

TORTURED SOUL

He got it from his grandmother on his 10th birthday. The acoustic was a Sears sunburst model and his fingers bled for months while he played and taught himself from old blues records.

Years passed. He graduated to a Fender Stratocaster and took the world by storm. He played until the notes were thoughts and the chords were ideas. He kept playing until the music supported his every move like a sonic skeleton.

Uncompromising, he never felt the need to be a part of the mainstream. He just played the blues. Everywhere, all the time, with total immersion and boundless passion.

Offstage he needed to recreate the thrill somehow but despite trying everything he never could. Sadly however, he did manage to destroy his health and create a monstrous habit.

One summer night his body collapsed onstage while he held a deep bend. People thought it was part of the show.

It wasn't.

*This film was a nice introduction to the passion and sincerity of an Irish Bluesman that remained kind and refused to be moved by anything other than his own heart and desire to play the music he had it in him to play.

Everyday Sunshine:

The Story of Fishbone

PERSEVERANCE

Never give up. Never stop. Always keep going. Compromise is not an option. Play the music however it comes. For the absolute love of it. No one, nothing, will get in the way of this steamroller. It has taken on a life of its own. Being recognized or validated takes a back seat to expression. The music, and the creation of it is all there is. Everything else is secondary.

Off the road and out of the studio life is hard. Not everyone likes or understands what they are trying to do. Most people still have no idea who they are. They must work regular jobs to subsist. From the machine gun power of shouting lyrics to asking: "Would you like fries with that?" is a fucking mindblower. How are they supposed to reconcile the two?

But they must. For that is the plight of the true musician. The original musician. The uncompromising one.

Prepare yourself creative types. Your road is going to be long. It is going to be arduous. Do not make the mistake of believing that it's going to be easy. No one owes you a thing. Even when you work hard.

"There are different types of success," a musician named Will Hoppey expressed to me years ago. Not everyone is a superstar. Not everyone wants to be.

*Fishbone epitomizes this idea. They are all true artists. This film was thoroughly inspiring. Especially for those creative types that are too far gone to give up now.

Albums Listened to for Metallic Inspiration Heading into Section 3:

1. Vader-Necropolis

2. Shinedown-Leave a Whisper

3. Terrorizer-Hordes of Zombies

4. Rage Against the Machine-Renegades

5. Iron Maiden-Killers, Number of the Beast, Piece of Mind, Somewhere In Time, Seventh Son of a Seventh Son, Brave New World

6. Judas Priest-Screaming for Vengeance, Sad Wings of Destiny, Stained Class, British Steel, Sin After Sin, Point of Entry, Redeemer of Souls

7. Black Sabbath-Sabbath Bloody Sabbath, Heaven and Hell, Mob Rules, Vol. 4 (Vol. 4 appears twice in this book because the album fucking destroys!)

8. Drowning Pool-Desensitized

9. Godsmack-Godsmack, Faceless, IV

10. White Zombie-La Sexorcisto Devil Music, Astro Creep 2000

11. Van Halen- Van Halen, Van Halen II, Women and Children First, Fair Warning, Diver Down, 1984

12. King Diamond-Abigail

13. Clutch-Jam Room

14. Steve Vai-Passion and Warfare, Sex and Religion

15. AC/DC-Dirty Deeds Done Dirt Cheap, Back In Black, For Those About to Rock

16. Scorpions-Lovedrive, Blackout

17. Mastodon-Blood Mountain, The Hunter

18. Ancestors-Of Sound Mind

19. Trapt-Trapt

20. Disturbed-Believe

21. Twisted Sister-You Can't Stop Rock and Roll, Stay Hungry

22. Linkin Park-Hybrid Theory

23. Megadeth-Countdown to Extinction, Killing Is My Business; And Business Is Good, Peace Sells But Who's Buying, Rust In Peace, So Far So Good...So What!!!

24. Audioslave-Audioslave

25. Marilyn Manson-Antichrist Superstar, Mechanical Animals, Holy Wood, The Golden Age of Grotesque

26. System of a Down-Toxicity

27. Ozzy-Diary of a Madman, Bark At the Moon, The Ultimate Sin

28. Dio-Holy Diver, The Last In Line, Sacred Heart

29. Static-X-Machine, Wisconsin Death Trip, Shadow Zone

30. Chevelle-Point #1

31. Staind-Tormented, 14 Shades of Grey, Staind

32. Lamb of God-Wrath, Resolution

33. Converge-Axe to Fall

34. Soulfly-Enslaved

35. Tool-Undertow, Aenema, Lateralus

36. Korn-Life Is Peachy, Issues

37. Queensryche-Operation Mindcrime, Empire, Promised Land

38. Metallica-Master of Puppets, Ride the Lightning, Death Magnetic, Beyond Magnetic

39. Fuel-Natural Selection

40. The Red Chord-Fed Through the Teeth Machine

41. Overkill-The Electric Age

42. Meshuggah-Koloss

43. Go Forth-Mindful

44. Johnny Cash-American III Solitary Man

I don't expect you to but I heartily recommend listening to all of the listed albums. Although I thoroughly enjoy all types of music and I always try to listen without prejudice, it always seems to go back to the heavy for me.

The next section describes that progression. That mindset. Where all of life's worries and assorted other bullshit disappears in searing riffs, soaring (or guttural) vocals, and the heavy bottom combination of bass and drums.

What would life be like without the heart pounding release of the heavy? Probably a lot more insane and violent.

Git some!

Section 3:

FULL METAL RACKET

1. VINYL INTRODUCTION

I remember sort of walking around in a semi-pleasant daze. Except when my old man was kicking my ass that is. Then I was just scared. But slowly music was coming into my life. With each note, each song, each new sonic discovery things seemed to be getting better. Somehow more hopeful.

I had begun my musical education in the car like many american kids. It seemed like we were always in the car, and there was always some form of music playing. My mother listened to Anne Murray, Kenny Rogers, Carly Simon, Liza Minelli, and a bevvy of film soundtracks from West Side Story to Grease. My father (when he wasn't reaching back to slap me) sang along to Elvis, Janis Joplin, and other hits of the day like America's "Horse With No Name," and a few crooners like James Taylor or maybe Frank Sinatra.

It wasn't a huge record collection at home but there were a few gems. The first Beatles record was in there as well as Sgt. Pepper's. I also remember Chicago and Michael Jackson's Off the Wall. But nothing compared to my 10th Christmas.

That Christmas of my 10th year was magic. I got my first album. It was Bruce Springsteen's The River and it was all mine. I tore into that square shaped package then the plastic wrap and immediately found the song "Hungry Heart" with the needle. It was amazing. I loved that song! Played it over and over again that Christmas morning and all my troubles just disappeared. This was it! I had found the mysterious ingredient to happiness. Did anyone else know about this? Music. Plain and simple. Music was the answer. Wake up the neighbors! Now I understood. And I wanted to share it. So I turned it up.

Way up. I wanted everyone to hear! In a flash I felt a big hand bounce off the back of my head and my father's voice boomed:

"Turn this shit down you asswipe, you wanna go fucking deaf?!"

Another beautiful moment ruined. The magic cut short once again. But my monumental discovery would never be forgotten. The damage had already been done. I was a music fan.

In time I found many willing accomplices to tend to my new addiction. Many friends and family members stoked the musical fires. My second album was given to me as a birthday present by my uncle, an amateur drummer and already a full time drunk and drug addict. Lynyrd Skynyrd-Second Helping opened the door even further. The Ballad of Curtis Loew, Swamp Music, and of course Sweet Home Alabama just floored me. I had never heard a band like that before. They were BAD.

The following Christmas I requested AC/DC's Back In Black. To my surprise my father bought it for me. He had no idea what lay behind that pitch black album sleeve because if he did he would have never even picked it up. Thank you nondescript packaging. I put that one on the turntable and fully expected to receive a shot in the chops. Instead my father just shook his head and showed his utter contempt for yet another thing that I liked. "That degenerate can't sing. He sounds like he's gargling glass for Chrissakes," was all Mr. Support could manage. But when the first strains of Hells Bells rose through the speakers I knew right then and there that his approval would never be needed again. His hold over me was finished. I think that was why he hated my music. Because it represented freedom and he had lost his when I was born.

Later the next year he checked out early at the ripe old age of 33. Everyone was devastated. I was relieved. No more beatings. No more fear. I could listen to whatever the fuck I wanted. I was free! There. I said it. The man was not a good father. But neither was the next guy.

My stepfather did less than nothing for me. He was a high school friend of my mother and father's who hung around like a creep and capitalized on my father's death and my mother's fear and grief. But that motherfucker had a killer record collection boy. And in it one fine day I found the album that changed everything.

I slid it out and was immediately struck by the ornate artwork, and the dark somewhat scary name of this mysterious group. Black Sabbath-Sabbath Bloody Sabbath turned me instantaneously into a heavy music fan. I was now a heavy music fan. I was now a metalhead, and would be until my dying day.

Then came Priest followed closely by Maiden, et al. I surrounded myself with music when I was a kid. My Uncle was a great amateur drummer and was in a few bands. My cousin was a famous producer but also a selfish active drug addict that never helped anyone in the family because he was too busy being Mr. Big. Another cousin used to play guitar at all family functions. Still another younger cousin used to play accordion and there were my own aborted attempts at violin, clarinet, sax, and later guitar. My first and second guitars both got Pete Townshended out of sheer frustration. I suppose I wasn't meant to be a musician, just a music appreciator. There was no one who appreciated music more than I. I could literally get drunk on it. Feelings of awe and ecstasy went through me while listening.

I was quite literally in love.

2. MESMERIZATION/AWAKENING

Judas Priest, Iron Maiden, Dio. There were many shows over the years but these bands stand out.

My first show was Quiet Riot and Iron Maiden at Radio City Music Hall. I was instantly mesmerized. I stood with my mouth agape for the better part of 2 hours. Nothing could break through. I found out what I wanted to do. This was it. I was going to be onstage if it killed me. Then some idiot squirted a can of lighter fluid on a row of seats and lit it on fire. Everyone was evacuated but the damage had been done. I was wide awake, and didn't sleep for 2 solid days.

The Priest shows that stand out are the one at Madison Square Garden where the crowd ripped the place apart and Judas Priest were banned from the Garden forever.

And the concert in Maryland where I went backstage because a friend of a friend died in a car accident. The band's management found out about the kid's death and furnished his Mom and about 30 of his friends with tickets. It was a great night. I kept stealing glances at the boy's mother all decked out in leather, dancing, crying, and celebrating her son's life. Meeting Rob Halford paled in comparison to this woman's devotion to her dead son.

And of course there was the Dio show at the old Philadelphia Spectrum. 3 friends bailed out on me at the last minute. I said fuck it, and went alone. I'm so glad I did. No one felt music the same way I did anyway. Standing there with 20,000 strangers watching and listening to a master vocalist something clicked. I was going to be a singer. I could do this. It was the first thing I was absolutely sure of.

The only other significant event from this time was the desire to have a painted denim jacket. It was almost synonymous with being the lead singer in a band to me. I had friends who had the covers of Priest, Maiden, Dio, Rush, Zepellin, and other album covers painted perfectly on the backs of their jean jackets. I was so jealous. And I lacked the princely sum of 100 dollars to get my own done. Money was something that was always tied up in essentials. There was never any left over for wants, desires, or luxuries. My father was dead and I was a reluctant contributor to my shattered family. This made me an angry young man.

Very angry.

I could not reconcile how I was going to be a provider for my 4 sisters and little brother and become a singer. So after high school I began running. It was selfish of me. But I'd get to them once I reached my goal.

I joined the U.S. Navy and was off to bootcamp in the freezing cold Great Lakes region in the dead of winter 1985.

3. PERFORMING

The Navy was an absolute bust. I forgot to take into consideration that I really didn't like anyone telling me what to do. Suddenly everyone was telling me what to do. Not good. 2 years into my 4 year enlistment I was home. But that's a whole other story.

I was at my mother's house for approximately 3 weeks and I couldn't take it anymore. Total insanity, absence of logic, a full fledged drunk without the drinking. I had to boogie. Hollywood here I come.

I thought a lot about Hollywood and figured it was the place to be for a heavy metal musician. I bought a greyhound bus ticket and rode 3 full days cross country. My feet were covered in jungle rot by the time I made it out there. And it took me a whole fucking week to recover from the bus ride.

As I recovered a plan took shape in my head. I would audition at the Guitar institute of technology and become one of the pre-eminent metal guitarists of all time. I thought big. Or dreamed big rather. Did it really matter that I could barely play?

Needless to say, that never happened. I just kept dreaming and drinking and soon I was penniless, homeless, and subsisting on pizza crusts and half eaten submarine sandwiches out at the Venice beach boardwalk.

A friend's parents paid for me to get back to New York and I was grateful yet embarrassed. I thought the sonofabitch was gonna lend me his money, not his mommy and daddy's, or I never would have asked. And he showed up at the airport with the both of them! Come on pal. Help me out here. A bit of common sense please? But he was a great friend despite his tight assedness. This same friend introduced me to the guitar player (a friend of his from college) that would start me off on my performance journey.

First there was a classic rock band. We never had a proper name. We just jammed for hours and I worked on my vocal chops belting out tunes like; For What It's Worth, White Room, Cortez the Killer, and a little light Sabbath. This group lasted about a year but when the guitar player and I discovered that no one but us had any plans of performing live, it was over.

What came next was one of the greatest experiences of my life. For 2 solid years the heavy metal band Demonaut dominated much of my time and effort. I became their lead singer/frontman.

Demonaut consisted of myself on lead vocals, Dominick on guitar, Mike on the other guitar, Tommy on bass, and Donny on drums. And for the first time in my life I felt like this was exactly where I belonged.

We started out doing covers of our favorite heavy metal and hard rock bands. Songs like; Hellion/Electric Eye by Priest. The Trooper by Maiden. For Whom the Bell Tolls by Metallica. Mob Rules by Sabbath with Dio, etc. We covered tunes until we had them down exactly. We were all perfectionists. Sometimes to a fault. Then we began writing and that was really where I found my groove. I was a good lyricist. Give me any piece of heavy music and I could put words to it. It felt like fucking magic.

Arbeit Macht Frei was a Maidenesque song about the holocaust. The Butcher's Theater was a song about a serial killer that had growling and screaming in it way before it was fashionable. The Silent Knight was a song about an apocalyptic warrior and we wrote many others in varying stages of completion.

The band was a juggernaut. Those who saw us loved us. I replaced a singer by the name of Henry who apparently couldn't sing at all. When I auditioned for the band at a studio in N.Y. they had me sing a difficult Judas Priest tune called Victim of Changes. When I came out of the vocal booth everyone was smiling and the engineer exclaimed; "Holy Shit!" Henry was Tommy the bass player's semi-bro in law because Tommy was dating Henry's sister. That was the only reason Henry ever played with Demonaut in the first place, because he really was fucking horrible. I was the last piece of the puzzle. "Now you have a fucking metal band boys," shouted the engineer. "This motherfucker can sing!"

So we played. We rehearsed, practiced, wrote, played live, everything a young band is supposed to do. But some band members were more committed than others. I happened to be a committed one. And the members that were just fucking around drove me nuts.

Tommy the bass player was under the bitchy spell of Henry's insane sister. He would walk out of practice following after her like a trained dog. Donny the drummer's girlfriend was more subtle but she was a pain in the ass too. Dominick was under the spell of a little whackjob Filipino chick that everyone started to refer to as Yoko Oh No! And I of course had gotten the French chick pregnant. At the time she was supportive though. She wanted to be married to a professional musician. She knew what it meant moneywise.

No matter how hard I tried to hold on Demonaut was destined to fail. My ambition far outweighed that of my bandmates. They didn't want it like I did. They weren't prepared to sacrifice. And that was a damn shame. Because the talent was there. We could all feel it when we played.

I knew it.

It was hard to let it go.

Seemed like such a waste.

But we all walked away nevertheless. I wonder if they think about it like I do. Of what could have been. All we needed was discipline and drive. They lacked both. But the single thing that killed the band for sure was lack of belief.

We were good fellas.

Really good.

Why couldn't you believe?

I did.

4. NO OUTLET

I walked away from the band angry but thoroughly unaware. I truly did not know that I was severing the one thing that was keeping me from losing my mind. The only thing I was thinking was that I couldn't continue to be associated with people who didn't take shit seriously.

During my travels I saw something that speaks volumes about this period. I attended a death metal festival in Montreal, Canada and sitting docile heavily chained at the base of the monitors were several muscular pit bulls. I asked a guy didn't the loud, extreme music bother the poor animals? He said: "No. Heavy music actually soothes them.

I had taken the one thing that soothed me and removed it from my life. Music had tamed my savage beast within. Loud, heavy, extreme, it grounded me and took care of my aggressive tendencies. I do suspect that there would be a lot of dangerous animals out there without metal. This music doesn't cause violence. It prevents it.

It started with a simple argument. I was in a deli picking up lunch when a loud asshole complained about me taking too long to order. I slit his throat with a box cutter in the parking lot and left him half in, half out of his car to die. That was the beginning. There were many attacks after that but you always remember your first. It's always the clearest.

Roaming the countryside I killed pretty much at will. It always seemed to be the assholes. The rude ones. The clueless disrespectful fools who believed they could treat others however they felt like.

I stomped out a loudmouthed teen behind a dumpster for letting a 7-11 door slam in an elderly woman's face. "Ya snooze, ya lose bitch," he said to her. He snoozed and lost. I was picking teeth and tiny jagged skull fragments out of my boot soles for weeks.

A man was pulled over on the side of an off ramp and I found him beating on his woman. The papers said his remains were found tied to a tree in the woods. I eviscerated him and tied him to a tree with his own entrails, so technically the papers were right. I suppose the animals got the rest.

Whenever something or someone triggered my anger I simply reacted. There was absolutely no soundtrack to these horrific acts. They took place as though in a silent movie. Dramatic but lackluster.

An owner mistreated his dog. I took the leash and hung him from a chain link fence. His dog sat still and watched him die.

A man was raping a young girl. I held him down while she actually took care of him. After she chopped off the offending member and I watched her throw it down a sewer drain, she hesitated. "It's alright," I whispered to her, then she stabbed him in the chest 17 times.

There were many more. Far too many to list here. I was untethered and had no way to express myself except through violence. I desperately needed an outlet or I was going to get caught. I could feel it coming.

Amidst all of this madness my son was born. The miracle of his birth was not lost on me. Despite the utter insanity I was perpetuating the joy I felt was real. Witnessing his birth up until that point was the greatest moment of my life. As I held his tiny body in my arms I believed that this was it. The missing link. How could I ever commit an act of violence again and return to hold him?

Shortly after placing him back in his bassinette and kissing his sleeping mother's forehead I was slamming an extra rude car valet's neck repeatedly in the trunk of my car because he told me to go fuck myself.

So not even the birth of my son could soothe the savage beast within.

I went home that night and began slowly listening to music again. As more time passed the heavier it got. I began writing about the music I was listening to. Inventing stories for the songs I was hearing. I visited the hospital daily, wrote nightly, and discovered something extremely important. As I wrote the violence stopped. There were many instances of rudeness and disrespect but they were written about and went unpunished. I came to the dramatic realization that I must produce art or the worst comes out.

Guaranteed.

Since I had left the band I had explored no other artistic outlet. In neglecting to do so I had become a hyper-sensitive lunatic ready to snap at a moment's notice.

I wrote and worked and raised my son to the best of my ability. I had other children and did the same. My first born ironically became a successful hardcore musician. A screamer of satanic proportions. He signed a record deal, put out a fine album, and performed countless shows. I was and am very proud of him. I've tried to steer him away from some mistakes I had made, but in the end I realize he has his own thing. He will succeed or fail on his own merit. It's got nothing to do with me.

My son possesses many of the same violent tendencies as his father. But he releases them onstage with his band. I pray he continues. Then he'll never have to choose between violent acts or writing. Fiction or reality.

He'll never have to let the reader be the judge.

The music itself will always be enough.

OUTRO:

There are countless clips, videos, albums, and songs that are not listed here that I pored over and enjoyed immensely during the writing of this book. I couldn't possibly include all of them here. The sheer amount would require several volumes.

One thing I learned listening intently to so many different genres is that it doesn't have to be metal to be "heavy". As evidenced by the one and only man in black. His last work was rich, devastating, and as "heavy" as any music could ever get. Johnny Cash is as they say; a fucking beast!

However, nothing I or anyone else creates, no piece of art, writing, or music will ever compare to the beauty and perfection I was blessed with by becoming a father. I surely did not deserve it, but it happened.

I have been there for all of my children through thick and thin. I have sacrificed more than I could ever explain or care to. And I haven't been the same since. I am a much better man because of them. They are all Miniature Symphonies in their own right.

I now have a 24 year old son, a 23 year old daughter who is pregnant (Grandpa time!), two 21 year old daughters, a 17 year old daughter, a 16 year old son, and a little 5 year old daughter who keeps me young. But I am not young. I am OLD! An aging Metalhead surrounded by family and love. Could there be anything better?

My children showed me what kind of man I really was. How strong I could be.

They defined me.

They saved my life.

I will always love them.

That being said; Love does not equal weakness.

Blood should always equal loyalty.

Catch that drift?

Probably not.

But a man can hope.

Keep listening.

The truth is always revealed through music.

F.J. Gouldner

Jersey Shore

Post Sandy

2014

www.fjgouldner.com

18591375R00086

Made in the USA
Middletown, DE
13 March 2015